Women's Role in World Religions

Comparative Religion: Exploring the Historical and Contemporary Role of Women in Major Religious Traditions

Water Tree Publishing

Table of Contents

Introduction

Religion is one of the most complicated and interesting topics to discuss in the world. This holds true no matter which religion you are talking about. Judaism, Christianity, Islam, Buddhism, and even Wicca. Whatever your faith may be, that religion plays a significant role in shaping people's lives is an undeniable fact. This is part of the reason why scholars upon scholars have devoted their lives to understanding religious experience. Yet these scholars' explanations and explorations of religious experience have been rather incomplete. This is because few, if any, scholars really took the time and effort needed to study women's role and place in religion and religious experience. This is incredibly problematic because women make up half the world's population. Not only that but religion often has the biggest impact on how women govern their lives and understand their own place in the world.

Imagine that you are standing before a painting. One side of this painting has been completely covered up with a blank sheet. The other side is fully visible. Later that day, a friend asks you about the painting you saw. So, you dive into an explanation of it, trying to describe the whole of the work without having seen it in its entirety. After all, you think to yourself, the covered-up left side of the canvas must be exactly the same as the visible right side, right? Unbeknownst to you, though, the left side of the painting is completely different from the right side. It is filled with all sorts of new colors, symbols, and uses brushstrokes in new, unheard-of ways before.

Trying to understand a religion—any religion—without comprehending women's place and role in it is like trying to describe a painting without fully seeing it, then. You can give it the old college try, of course, and you may even get some points right by pure chance and guesswork. However, you are going to get a great many things wrong and, in the process, come to see religion as something other than what it actually is. If we want to truly understand the religions we believe in, then we have to make an effort to understand women's role in them as well. Only in doing so can we lift the veil that has been drawn before our eyes.

My desire to remove this veil from our eyes is the very reason why I have decided to write *Women's Role in World's Religions*. On the whole, *Women's Role in World's Religions* looks at four major religious traditions: Abrahamic Religions, Eastern Religions, Indigenous Religions, and New Religious Movements. In the process, it strives to explore the real role that women have played throughout centuries and generations in religious practices. It seeks to discover the leadership roles women took on in their faiths, whether we realize it or not. Aside from that, *Women's Role in World's Religions* strives to understand whether the roles that women play in their faiths have changed in any way over the years or not. It tries to understand how women's roles have changed, too, with the passing of the centuries in a world that seems to be becoming increasingly secular.

A lot of people, too many people, in fact, operate under the assumption that women have never held any leadership positions in the world of faith. Despite what these nonbelievers think, though, there have been numerous women leaders in a variety of different religions. The many examples we will see in this book, from Deborah and Miriam to Khadija and Sun Ba-Er, prove as much. These women have played a crucial role in the shaping of their own beliefs and those of others. A woman in a leadership role? Heaven forbid! Well, actually, heaven has not exactly forbidden this, as a quick look at religious history would prove. It can even be said that heaven, or whatever alternative to heaven you believe in, has permitted this. The women leaders that have thus come into the religious sphere have had a major hand in the shaping of the lives of women. In the process, they have come to shape the cultures we have grown up in, along with the gender expectations that are upon us in our societies and the realities that we live in, be they good, bad, or something in between.

Understanding women's role in religions is a necessary undertaking for anyone who wishes to understand their own reality as well. This holds true for everyone, from the most faithful of believers to staunch atheists. The fact of the matter is our religions have been shaping our cultures and lives for many years. It is only by coming to grasp them, then, that we can really see the full picture of the world we live in. It is only then that we can grasp our own place in that world too. Only by unveiling that second half of the painting can we really take in the glory of the full, finished masterpiece before us. With that in mind, the question remains: Are you ready to take a peek?

Part I:

Women in Abrahamic Religions

Chapter 1:

Women in Judaism

There are many different religions in the world, as you probably know. One of these religions is known as Judaism. Judaism, like Christianity and Islam, is an Abrahamic religion. That means it is a belief system centered around worshiping the God of Abraham. Why Abraham? Well, it is because Abraham is said to be the founder of Judaism. That does not mean he created Judaism, of course, but rather that he was the first person God chose to reveal the faith to. Before we can come to understand the role that women have played in Judaism over the years, we must first understand what Judaism is. What on earth is this religion truly about? How did it come to be, and why is it so important? Well, let's find out.

A Quick History of Judaism

Judaism is a monotheistic religion, meaning that it states there is only one God to believe in, as opposed to many. It is considered to be the oldest monotheistic religion in the world, dating back some 4,000 years (*Judaism*, 2018)! According to Judaism, thousands of years ago, God made a special agreement, which is officially known as a covenant with His believers. Today, we refer to the followers of Judaism as "Jewish people." However, Jewish people did not start calling themselves that until around the year 500 B.C.E. (Ahuvia, n.d.). But hey, what is in a name? Jewish people are descended from the Ancient Israelites, who themselves believed they were descended from three specific people: Abraham, Abraham's son Isaac, and Isaac's son Jacob.

The sacred text of Jewish people is the Hebrew Bible, otherwise known as the Torah, which means "teaching." According to one story from the Torah, Ancient Israelites were forced to Ancient Egypt when their lands were struck with a terrible drought. Sadly, they were enslaved when they got to Egypt and labored away for many years. It was only when God sent the Israelites a prophet called Moses, along with several plagues to force the Egyptian Pharaoh's hand, that the Ancient Israelites obtained their freedom. Once they were freed, the Israelites and Moses departed Egypt and made it back to the "Promised Land," which is said to be the lands where Abraham, his son Isaac, and his grandson Jacob all used to live.

So, what happened after Jewish people arrived at the Promised Land? Well, they were ruled by King David for some time, whose son Solomon built the first-ever Jewish Temple. This was in the years of 1000 B.C.E. (*Judaism*, 2018). This temple was sadly destroyed by the Babylonian in 587 B.C.E., and while it was rebuilt, it was destroyed yet again by the Ancient Romans.

The Core Beliefs of Judaism

The history of Judaism goes on from there, of course, and features many interesting stories, as well as wars and struggles. The point, however, is this: Judaism is one of the oldest religions in the world and, as such, has been shaping the lives of both individuals and entire communities for many centuries. The core beliefs of Judaism can be summed up as follows (*Religions—Judaism: Jewish beliefs*, 2009):

- There is only one God that created the entire universe. Any individual human being can have a personal relationship with God, and God is still involved in the workings of the world, influencing everything that happens.

- God established a covenant with the Jewish people, which states that they must continually work for the Jewish people in exchange for the good deeds that God does for them.

- In keeping with that, Jewish people must seek to bring the divine into everything that they do, and they must obey God's laws.

- Jewish people are God's chosen people.

- Judaism is a family faith, which means that religious ceremonies begin as early as when a baby is only eight days old. Given that many Jewish religious practices and traditions, like the Sabbath meal, revolve around the home.

Seeing as the subject matter of this book and the traditional link between family life and women, that last belief is especially important. With that in mind, what is the role of the Jewish woman in her own faith? How has this role evolved or changed over the years, and how has Judaism shaped women's lives?

Women's Role in Traditional Judaism

We have to look at religion from two specific lenses when considering women's role in it. First, we must consider things within the historical context they have occurred in. Second, we must adopt a more contemporary lens and see how certain concepts and practices have evolved and changed over time. When we do not consider matters in their original historical context, we fail to understand them properly. For instance, there is a great deal of misconceptions about women's role in traditional Judaism in the day and age that we live in. A lot of contemporary readers seem to believe that women occupied a lowly status in traditional Judaism. This, however, was not the case.

Jewish people have their own set of laws that they abide by. This set of laws is known as Halakah, and it dates all the way back to Biblical times. If you look at Halakhah through a contemporary feminist lens, you will be forced to conclude that women had a lowly role in Judaism. However, if you look at Halakhah through a historical lens, you will see that women's role in religion at the time was much better than, say, the societal position they held under American civil rights in the 1800s (Rich, n.d.). That is a little bit insane when you think about it.

So, how exactly did traditional Judaism treat women? For starters, traditional Judaism saw women as "different from" but "equal to" men. They had different responsibilities to play in the family and society itself, but they were no less important than men were. One of the most important bits of evidence proving that traditional Judaism considered men and women equal is that Jewish people believe that God is neither male nor female. Instead, Jewish people maintained that God possessed both male and female qualities. Since human beings were created in the image of God, a lot of religious scholars think that they were originally created as dual-gendered beings. Over time, however, they separated into two different beings—man and woman—and still exist in those two forms.

Since Judaism considers men and women to be different but equal, it can be said that it ascribes different qualities to them too. For example, women are said to have more "*binah*" in them than men. In Judaism, binah means understanding, intelligence, and intuition. This is presumably why they did not commit an act of sin by worshiping the Golden Calf after Moses went to Mt. Sinai. Only the men did that.

As the story goes, the ancient Israelites were waiting around for Moses to come back, but unfortunately, Moses was taking his sweet time. Losing faith a bit, they turned to Moses' brother Aaron and asked him to make them a new God (Nelson, 2020). Aaron obliged by collecting everyone's golden earrings, melting them down, and using the mixture to make a Golden Calf. Satisfied with the results, the men took the calf and began worshiping it. This came to an abrupt end, though, when Moses came back. Upset at what his brethren were doing, Moses took the idol, melted it back down, pulverized it, threw the remains in the water, and then made the sinners drink that matter. Was this overkill? Maybe a little. Did it get the message across? Certainly!

Another example of male and female equality in traditional Judaism is how the 10 Commandments demand that both fathers and mothers be respected by their children. Some may argue that while that may be the case, Exodus 20:12 names fathers before naming mothers. This argument, which hints at an imbalance between men and women, can be countered with the fact that mothers are named before fathers in Leviticus 19:3, which shows that mothers and fathers should be treated with the same amount of dignity and respect (*Holy Bible: Containing the Old and New Testaments, Leviticus 19:3*, n.d.).

Still, another example of the respect shown to women in traditional Judaism is the fact that there were women who actually occupied significant leadership positions in Judaism. The stories of these women effectively illustrate the main characteristics ascribed to women by Judaism, the roles they were expected to play in society, and the responsibilities they had to bear as a result.

Women Leaders in Judaism

The first name on our list of Judaic leaders and heroines is Miriam. Miriam is Moses' and Aaron's sister and, interestingly enough, one of the few, if not only, Judaic heroines that is never referred to as a mother or wife (Trible, 1999). But more on that later. Miriam initially helps save her brother Moses' life by delivering him onto the Nile River. In Exodus 15:20–21, Miriam is referred to as "Prophet Miriam, Aaron's sister" and thus becomes the first woman in the Bible to bear that title (*Holy Bible: Containing the Old and New Testaments, Exodus 15:20–21* n.d.).

This makes a great deal of sense when you consider her later actions. It is Miriam, after all, who leads Hebrew women in song, dance, and the playing of drums. It is also Miriam who actively challenges Moses' authority along the march to the Promised Lands. This happens when Miriam asks if Moses is the only one God has spoken through and emphasizes that He has spoken through herself and her brother Aaron as well (Sulomm, 2006).

Unfortunately, Miriam pays a high price for speaking out in this way. Soon, she's struck by an ailment where she becomes covered in scales. Miriam endures a lot of pain because of this punishment, and Aaron pleads with Moses on her behalf. Moses, in turn, pleads with God. So, it is that the scales disappear, and Miriam is confined somewhere outside the camp they are all in for seven days as an alternative punishment. It is interesting to note that Miriam and Aaron both challenge Moses' authority, but it is only Miriam that is punished for this action. The message given here, then, is all too clear: While women may occupy roles of leadership, they cannot challenge the authority of a man, though other men are free to do so. It is not surprising, then, that Miriam never speaks so much as a single word after her punishment is over, nor is it surprising that others stop speaking to her.

Coming from the same people that refused to continue on with their march until Miriam's health was restored, this seems like an odd thing to do, does it not? Yet small controversies like that are not all that uncommon. For instance, Miriam dies without anyone ever speaking a single word to her again. Yet, when she dies, all the wells across the desert suddenly dry up as though nature itself wants to honor her. Centuries after her passing, Miriam is remembered as Moses and Aaron's equal.

Sarah, one of the four Jewish matriarchs, is another significant heroine with much to tell us. Sarah was Abraham's wife and half-sister since incest was not considered to be as cringeworthy those days as it it is now. She was one of the four most beautiful women in the world and was, in fact, the most beautiful among them. Unfortunately, she was also barren (Kadari, 1999a). Unlike with most women, though, Sarah's barrenness was not seen as a God-given punishment. This probably has to do with the fact that she did get pregnant at the age of 90 as a reward for her many good deeds.

Now, you might be thinking, how is pregnancy at 90 years old a reward? Well, Sarah's pregnancy was a reward for two reasons. First, she really, really wanted to have a child. Second, according to Judaism, a woman's primary role is to be a mother and a wife. As such, the greatest gift a woman can receive is a child of her own, or so we are told. Of course, there is also the fact that Sarah's youth was restored to her when she finally got pregnant, which undoubtedly helped a lot.

Getting back into it, according to Rabbis, Sarah was a prophet, just like Miriam. This is why God specifically told Abraham to do whatever Sarah tells him to do in Genesis 21:12 (*Holy Bible: Containing the Old and New Testaments.*, *Genesis 21:12*, n.d.). Unlike most Judaic heroines, it was her husband Abraham who was ennobled through her, not the other way around. Aside from being very beautiful, Sarah is known to be incredibly virtuous.

As the story goes, Sarah and Abraham travel to Egypt when a famine strikes their lands. Upon arriving, Sarah is forcibly taken to the Pharaoh, who thinks that only he should be allowed to have such a beautiful woman, not the husband she's happily married to. Sarah begs and protests, and when that does not work, she pleads with God for help. God obliges by sending her an angel who strikes and smites the Pharaoh whenever he tries to touch her and at her command. So, it is that Sarah's virtue remains intact. Eventually, she is allowed to return to her husband, and the two dwell in Canaan.

Of course, this story gives women another important message about the role they are supposed to play: Women are expected to be loyal to their husbands at all times and completely pure and virtuous. Despite how virtuous Sarah was, she was infertile, which, again, is usually considered to be a punishment for women. How does that work, then? Well, to start, Sarah Abraham tries for 10 years to have kids after they get to Canaan to no effect. So, Abraham takes a second wife, Hagar. Hagar was Sarah's maid, and it was Sarah who told Abraham to make her his second wife. She does this both because she wants kids and because she places Abraham having a son over all other desires. This, again, highlights the importance of women's roles as mothers.

Sarah's relationship with Hagar and the sons the two ultimately bear points to some interesting facts about women's roles as well. Hagar is known to treat Sarah very poorly, you see, to the point where she starts rumors about her behind her back. Sarah, however, does not reciprocate, nor does she descend to Hagar's level. Despite this, Hagar gets pregnant immediately, and it takes Sarah over 10 years to get pregnant herself. Yet Hagar's pregnancy does not turn out to be a blessing that pregnancies usually are depicted as because Hagar's son, Ishmael, turns out to be a bad egg. Sarah's son Isaac, on the other hand, turns out to be an exemplary son. Sarah and Hagar's story, then, shows how women are supposed to conduct themselves. The message here is clear: Be kind, selfless, and patient, and you will be rewarded. Be malicious, gossipy, and impatient, and you will be punished.

Our final Judaic heroine, though there are many others, is Deborah. Deborah was a prophet, too (Kadari, 1999a). She is the wife of Lappidoth, and she teaches her husband the Torah herself. Her prophetic abilities and her wisdom, for which she was known, were said to be the rewards of her many good deeds. Uncharacteristically for most Jewish women, Deborah actually participated in a war that was waged against the then king of Canaan. Actually, Deborah not only participated in this war, which is known as the Battle of Tabor, but she actually led it side-by-side with her husband. On top of that, Deborah acted as a judge, again, alongside her husband. When she was not doing that, she would sit beneath a palm tree and teach the public the Torah.

Deborah's one fault was that she was a proud individual, which makes sense given all her accomplishments. It must not have made sense to higher powers, though, because Deborah eventually lost her prophetic abilities because of her pride and haughtiness. What did Deborah do to be seen as haughty, you ask? Why, she sent someone to fetch her husband when he was needed rather than go fetch him herself. Oh, the audacity! What does Deborah's story teach us about women's roles then? That women cannot act proud or act in a way that disturbs the power of the sexes. Think about it: For all that men and women are equal in Judaism, can you name a single male prophet who would lose his abilities because they sent someone to fetch their wife when she was needed and did not go to get her himself?

Jewish Women's Role in Society

As these stories of Jewish heroines clearly show, women's primary role in society is that of mother and wife. Women primarily exist in the domestic sphere in the Judaic world. However, because they are considered intelligent beings equal to men, even though they are in a subservient role to them, they are allowed to take part in economic activities that would be beneficial to their families and households (Baskin, n.d.). For example, women are allowed to engage in trade with other private individuals. This is why Jewish women have been able to work in a number of trades, crafts, and business enterprises for centuries. They have even been able to bring claims to courts, attend gatherings with other women, and participate in social activities.

That being said, they were not allowed to participate in things like religious services, religious studies, or higher education. This is primarily because it was believed that such practices would interfere with women's chief role, which is that of a mother and wife. At the same time, there have been a number of Rabbis that worried women would become too devoted to their spiritual pursuits (Rich, n.d.). Add to that how some Rabbis described women as lazy, jealous, gossipy, and vain, and it is easy to see how women were pushed and relegated to mostly the domestic sphere.

Again though, women were not entirely in their roles in Judaism. They had the right to own, buy, and sell property and enter into contracts with people. These were rights that their contemporaries did not have in, say, the 19th century. They had the right to express their opinions on their marriage prospects. Unlike a lot of other religions, sex was considered to be a woman's right, not a man's. Again, unlike some religions, men did not have the right to beat or mistreat their wives. Marital rape was not permitted in Judaism either, and women had a right to change their minds and say "no" in the middle of intercourse. If said "no" was ignored, that was also considered rape.

Looking at all this, it is clear to see that while men and women were not wholly equal, Judaism expected and demanded that women be treated with respect and honor so long as they fulfilled their roles. This is to be expected since women's role as child-bearers and mothers is sacred. That is why Judaism itself passes from mothers to children and not from fathers to children like in a lot of other religions. This sacredness may also be part of the reason why women are exempted from most religious duties. There are some exceptions, though. For instance, women are tasked with lighting the Shabbat candles. Shabbat is a religious rest day where practically no technology is used. Families typically spend the day together at home. Since the woman's primary space in Judaism is at home, it is more than understandable that this is one of the few religious duties they are tasked with, is it not?

Here's the thing about society, though: It changes with the times. The society we live in today, therefore, looks very different from the societies that Miriam, Sarah, and Deborah lived in. Naturally, Jewish women's roles changed right along with it. That is not to say that women are no longer expected to be wives and mothers—they are. It just means that the things women are allowed to do have expanded dramatically. The sphere in which women live and operate has thus changed. There are still plenty of women who exist just in the domestic sphere, but there are many more that have pushed the boundaries.

Jewish women started to push religious boundaries during the feminist Jewish movements of the 70s, 80s, and 90s (Fishkoff, 2011). Women led some fierce battles in these eras to do all sorts of things, like have more gender-neutral language be introduced to prayer books and be allowed to actually study the Torah. They similarly led major battles to pursue higher education and have, for the most part, succeeded. Some of these battles are still going on, though, or else have to be waged again and again until the message that women will not go back to old ways sinks in. Back in 2015, for example, a number of ultra-conservative Rabbis tried to ban women from pursuing college degrees and going to religious seminaries. Female students, even ultra-Orthodox ones, abjectly refused this decree.

Contrary to what some may have expected, students would not drop out of their college programs, and why should they? It is their understanding, after all, that Jewish women's role in the modern age cannot be confined to the home. It is one of true equality where women are allowed to pursue the lives they want while practicing their faiths or, at least, it should be.

Chapter 2:

Women in Christianity

There are three Abrahamic religions on the whole, and Christianity is one of them. Christianity is rather complex when it comes to women. On the one hand, there have been many, many women in the world who both helped spread Christianity across the globe and played a crucial part in making it what it is. On the other, it seemed like Christianity had some interesting things to say about women, particularly with regard to the original sin—*cough* Eve *cough*—and women's subsequent subservience to men. If we want to truly grasp their true role in Christianity, we must first disentangle these notions. Before we can do that, though, we must first take a quick look at the history of Christianity so that we have the context we need.

A Quick History of Christianity

Christianity, the largest religion in the world, made its debut on the world stage in the 1st century in the Middle East. Interestingly enough, Christianity came into being as a movement within Judaism (Stefon, 2019). Before we get ahead of ourselves, yes, that does mean that Jesus was, in fact, Middle Eastern. But that is beside the point. The point is that Christianity was essentially built around Jesus of Nazareth. More specifically, the religion was centered around the birth, death, and eventual resurrection of Jesus Christ, though it did not really start taking a massive hold until about a century after Jesus' death (*Christianity*, 2017). The core of the religion starts when Mother Mary gives birth to Jesus. This is an immaculate birth, as you know—more on that later.

The reason Christianity started taking hold after Jesus' death is that this is when his 12 disciples wrote the four gospels, which are found in the New Testament (Stefon, 2019). These gospels, known as the Gospel of Matthew, Mark, Luke, and John, respectively, served as people's main source of information about Jesus and Christianity. The Gospels put Jesus' birth somewhere in the 6 or 7 C.E. and state that it actually caused a riot in the Roman Empire against the governor of Quirinius. The birth of a Messiah will do that to you. They put his crucifixion, which was ordered by Pontius Pilate, around the years 29–30. Between those years, Jesus did many fascinating things like having an encounter with St. John the Baptist in a desert and preaching repentance and baptism to him, performing miraculous acts of healing while he preached, and entering Jerusalem during Passover. This was followed by the infamous Last Supper, after which he was betrayed by Judas. This led to his arrest and crucifixion, of course, which was followed by his resurrection three days later.

The Core Beliefs of Christianity

So, what exactly were Jesus' teachings, which became the core beliefs of Christianity, that led to his death? For starters, like Judaism, Christianity claimed there is only one God, which was blasphemous to the Romans of the time, who believed in numerous different Gods like

Neptune and Jupiter. This God is said to have created the earth and the heavens (*Christianity*, 2017). One slightly complicated part of this belief is that the divine godhead is divided into three parts in Christianity, these parts being the Father, meaning God himself, Son, meaning Jesus, and the Holy Spirit.

The second crucial belief of Christianity is that Jesus was God's own son, to who Mary gave a virgin birth to, and was the Messiah sent to the Earth to save the world. Not everyone believed this at the time, though, and thus, Jesus was killed on the cross. He accepted this death and thus offered forgiveness for humankind's sins. Three days later, he was resurrected and then ascended to heaven. Christians further believe that one day, Jesus will return to earth, and this will be the beginning of the Second Coming. Since Christianity was born inside Judaism, Christians follow the Old Testament. However, they follow the New Testament as well, which contains the Gospels.

Women's Role in Traditional Christianity

So, where was a woman's place in all this? In the past, historians believed that save for a few obvious exceptions like Eve, Mother Mary, and Mary Magdalene, women had little to no role to play in Christianity. Women believers were thus often thought to be relegated to supportive, subservient roles for the most part. In recent years, however, an array of female historians have risen to the forefront, and they have uncovered many women leaders in the history of Christianity. These women have played an incremental role in both the spread and development of the faith. Before we can take a closer look at these women, though, let's take a look at the typical heroines of Christianity and see what roles, responsibilities, and characteristics were ascribed to women through them.

The first story in the Bible to deal with women, their characteristics, and their role in the world is found in Genesis. This is the story of Adam and Eve, the first man and woman to ever be created. This story is likely familiar to you: God creates Adam and places him in the Garden of Eden. Adam looks rather lonely, though, so he creates Eve and places her there too. Here they are meant to lead their lives in perfect bliss so long as they obey one rule. This rule is that they must never eat the fruit of the Tree of Knowledge. I suppose the old adage, ignorance is bliss, holds true in this case.

At first, both Adam and Eve abide by this rule. But then the devil, disguised as a serpent, slithers up to Eve and either tempts or tricks her into eating the fruit. Once Eve does so and gets wise, she walks up to Adam and convinces him to have some of the fruit as well. Adam thinks, "Why not?" and eats the forbidden fruit. When God comes by the Garden of Eden and sees what happened, he becomes furious. Both Adam and Eve are expelled from the Garden of Eden thus and sent to Earth, where they will face many hardships. But that is not all, at least not for Eve. For she is given a second punishment: since she was the first one to eat the fruit and convince Adam to eat it as well, she must forever be subservient and obedient to man, be it her husband, her father, or a complete stranger. So, it was that Eve became the proverbial stick that was used to beat women for generations.

Here's the very interesting bit though: When Eve was originally created, she was created as a "helper" for Adam (Hamel, 2019). But what would Eve have to help Adam with somewhere as blissful as the

Garden of Eden? What was Eve's role, really? That of a secretary? A maid? A cook? Something else entirely? More to the point, how did Eve's role change after the couple was expelled from the Garden?

While we may never know what changed in Eve's designated role after the expulsion, we do know that the way she and all women thereafter were seen and treated changed. For instance, in 1 Timothy 2:12, it was stated that women should be silent in church (*Holy Bible: Containing the Old and New Testaments.*, *1 Timothy 2:12*, n.d.). This exact same thing was stated again in Corinthians 14:3 (*Holy Bible: Containing the Old and New Testaments.*, *Corinthians 14:3*, n.d.). Meanwhile, leading figures in the Christian church, like St. Paul, for instance, actively discouraged women from speaking their minds and enacting any sort of authority within the church.

We can derive a couple of things from this. The first is that the expulsion from the Garden was obviously blamed on Eve and women. As such, women were at best thought to be not wise enough to exercise any authority since they could fall into temptations and tempt others. They were relegated to the domestic sphere because of this and were expected to obey men—mainly their husbands and fathers—in all things. They were expected to be silent and in a position to continually repent for the original sin. This was part of women's role in Christianity as it was.

The second thing that can be derived from Eve's story is that women were always meant to be subservient to men. Eve was created to be a "helper" to Adam, after all. Given that, it can be argued that women's role in traditional Christianity was that of the "supporting best friend to the male lead."

Another heroine that Christian women are meant to look to in Christianity is Mother Mary. If Eve is the cautionary tale about how women should not behave—with authority and by exercising their curiosity and intellect—then Mother Mary is the golden standard they are meant to live by. To start with the most obvious, Mary is Jesus' mother and gave an immaculate birth. That means she was a virgin when she gave birth to Jesus (Roten, n.d.). The fact that Mary gives a virgin birth to the son of God says something very important and specific about women's sexuality: it should not exist.

We already know that there is a link between women and temptation, and thus, women and sin, thanks to Eve. Women's sexuality is an extension of that. As such, women's sexuality has long been seen as something bad and sinful in Christianity. True, women were still expected to be mothers and wives in Christianity. That was part of their primary role. However, they were not supposed to express their sexuality. Thus, unlike in Judaism, sex in marriage was the man's right, not the woman's. The woman was expected to free herself from such earthly temptation. She was supposed to be as pure as can be and seek to redeem herself for the original sin. This was part of her role. Hence, Mary's virgin birth.

Mary's purity is not the only thing that makes her Christianity's prescribed role model for women. For one, Mary was the prime example of what an obedient woman should look like. This is why she immediately accepts the mission she's given by God, as told to her by Archangel Gabriel: To bear the son of God. When Mary readily accepts her charge, Archangel Gabriel names her the handmaiden of the Lord, at least according to Luke 1:38 (Craven, 2018). Of course, part of Mary's obedience can be attributed to how devout a believer she was. That is another thing that traditional Christianity expected to be: faithful.

Mary has two other defining characteristics that Christianity would like for other women to have as well, for she is submissive and humble. Yet for all that Mary is submissive, she can also be described as brave. Think about it: Mary became pregnant with the son of God before she was officially married to Joseph. When she came forward with her pregnancy to Joseph, her soon-to-be husband could have very easily doubted her word and forsaken her. Sharing her news with Joseph, then, thus, took courage. So did having word of her pregnancy spread, given the loose tongues that would be wagged about her.

Mary's bravery does not end there, though. Mary was also courageous enough to flee to a country she did not know in order to save her child's life—an experience many immigrant women are familiar with in the times that we live in. Does all this mean, then, that Christianity expects women to be brave? In a sense, yes. They are expected to face a number of hardships and challenges and be steadfast before them. This takes a certain degree of bravery.

Those two virtues—bravery and submissiveness—may appear to be at odds with one another, at least to a certain extent. But that is emblematic of Christianity's outlook on women. On the one hand, Christianity does treat women as temptresses and sinners to a certain extent, thanks to Eve. On the other hand, it treats them with respect if they faithfully face the hardships that are thrown at them, the way it does Mother Mary. Add to that Jesus' sacrifice to forgive humankind's sins, including women's, and it seems that women can hold revered positions in Christianity. This is why many of Christianity's first converts were women, for example (Woods, 2019). It is also why a great deal of women were present for Jesus' crucifixion. It is even why Mary Magdalene was the first person to find Jesus' empty tomb and recognize his voice, thereby discovering his resurrection.

Mary Magdalena is yet another fascinating character in the Bible that gives women an important message: You can always repent from sin and lead a virtuous life. In all honesty, Mary Magdalene might be the most complex female character to be encountered in the Bible. There is a widely held belief that Mary Magdalene was originally a prostitute. This, however, is patently untrue (Carroll, 2006). Mary Magdalene was not a prostitute, but she was one of Jesus' followers. It can even be said that Mary Magdalene was one of Jesus' most faithful, if not the most faithful, followers. She was the only one to stay with him when Jesus' life was in mortal danger, for instance. She was present at Jesus' crucifixion, and again, it was she who discovered Jesus' resurrection and delivered the good news to others. Today, Mary Magdalene is recognized by many as a saint. So, how is it that a saint got branded a former prostitute?

This can be explained by people's attitudes toward women, I think, particularly ones that exercise some degree of authority, which Mary Magdalene does. She was the only one to remain with Jesus when he was in mortal danger, as I said, which is a fact that can be painted in a certain kind of light if you are so inclined. That the intentions, actions, and stories of women who hold a measure of power can be twisted to create a new narrative about them is nothing new. So, it is entirely possible that the same happened with Mary Magdalene. This twisting of the truth can even be seen as the hardships that women are expected to weather while holding onto their faith, just as Mary Magdalene did.

So, what does Mary Magdalene tell women about their prescribed roles in Christianity? Two specific things. The first is that they have to be devout in their belief, never straying from their path and offering support in every way they are able. This is why Mary was with Jesus when his life was in danger and why she did things like offer him financial support to aid his cause. The second is that they have to be resolute in the face of challenges, even when those challenges come in the form of slander and gossip. The key message here is clear: So long as you are brave and resolute, all will turn out well.

There is that word again: brave. This is a more subtle but still perceptible message that Christianity has been giving to women throughout the centuries. It is a message that some Christian women have taken to heart to undertake a task that is as daunting as it is massive: To remake the mold the world has been trying to make them fit into.

Christian Women's Role in the Contemporary World

The traditional role that Christianity had assigned women—that of the submissive, obedient, silent wife and mother—is no longer satisfactory to most women, even ones who are devout believers. Look at the political sphere, for instance, and there are women politicians who are faithful Christians. When asked if it is right for a woman to be in politics, they have precedent to point to in the form of Deborah, after all. Look at the church itself, too, and you will find a significant number of women pastors, reverends, and other such leaders there. These are all women who have decided to use their voices to make themselves heard, enact change, and the kind of meaningful, devout lives that they want to lead.

Considering the role that Christianity has ascribed to women, you may think that these women are revolutionaries and pioneers. You will be surprised to find out that this is only partly true, though, because there have actually been women who took leadership positions in the church before, albeit on a smaller scale (Rust, 2022). Aside from the obvious examples of Deborah and Miriam, there was Phoebe, who was a deaconess, Apphia, Nympha, and Chloe, who led their own house churches, Tabitha, who led a ministry…

The female leaders of our time, then, are simply exercising the same bravery that these women exhibited in the past to expand their roles. They still are devout believers, obviously, and thus identify with a number of the characteristics that Christianity ascribes to them, such as humility, which is not, in fact, a bad thing. However, they are also breaking the "helper" mold that their faith has crafted for women and redefining the expectations made of their genders.

Chapter 3:

Women in Islam

While Islam is a monotheistic and Abrahamic religion like Christianity, its view on women and their role is a little different than that of Christianity. In some ways, this view is often misunderstood, at least to a degree, and this has a little to do with the Western gaze with which the religion is looked on. To properly understand women's role in Islam, we must look at the religion with a neutral, as opposed to specifically Western, gaze. We must also consider Islam within the historical context in which it came into being. To do that, we must, as always, take a look at how Islam came to be and how it rose and spread throughout the world.

A Quick History of Islam

Islam first came into being in the year 610 C.E. in the Arabian Peninsula, which at the time was made up of many different tribes and, thus, was torn by tribal warfare (Singley, 2020). Judaism and Christianity both existed in the world by this point. As with these two religions, Islam began with a prophet. This prophet was named Mohammed, who was visited by Archangel Gabriel—yes, the same one who visited Mother Mary as he quite liked to travel. Thus, Mohammed was given a mission to spread the new revelation that had been given to him. Mohammed would continue to receive several revelations over the next 24 years. After his death, these revelations would be written down at last, and so the holy book of Islam, the Qur'an, would come to be.

Mohammad was born in Mecca and was married to a wealthy woman called Khadijha. Khadijha was the first person Mohammed converted to Islam. She was also a businesswoman and the one to propose to Mohammed, not the other way around. Hence, she was a very interesting figure, but more on her later. After receiving the first revelation, Mohammed worked to spread Islam and lived in Mecca for about 12 years. At the time, most of the people living in Mecca were pagans. This means that those who converted to Islam risked their lives in doing so (Razwy, 2013). For example, the father of the first family to accept Islam, Yasir, was tortured by the pagans for doing so, and so were his wife and son.

This conflict between the Muslims and the Pagans eventually caused Mohammed and his followers to leave Mecca and head to Medina. This migration came to be known as the Hijah (Singley, 2020). This was not the end of things, though, as a series of battles followed between the Muslims and the pagans, ending in the Muslims' ultimate victory.

The Core Beliefs of Islam

As with Judaism and Christianity, Islam states that there is only one God to believe in. This is one of the five pillars of the faith. The other four are (Canby, 2021)

- That Muslims must pray five times a day, every day, facing the direction that Mecca is in. This prayer involves reacting to the first revelation in the Qur'an—these revelations are known as "*surahs*"—and is done on a prayer mat. This prayer is officially known as the *Salat*.

- That Muslims must donate a designated portion of what they earn every year to help those in need. This donation is known as paying *zakat*. Wealthy Muslims must build mosques, hospitals, schools, and other important institutions on top of paying zakat.

- That Muslims must fast during the ninth month of the Islamic calendar if they are healthy enough to go without food or drink for the day. This is done so that they do not take the blessings that have been given to them by God for granted, and so they empathize with those in need to a greater extent and, thus, become more willing to help them.

- That all Muslims who are able to visit Mecca, a holy city in Islam, at least once if their health and financial position allow them to do so. This visit is known as the *Hajj*.

Women's Role in Islam

Overall, there seems to be some disagreements and even controversy regarding women's role in Islam. This is because some of the clauses regarding women in the Qur'an seem to clash with one another a bit. In the first verse of the An-Nisaa chapter of the Qur'an, for instance, it is stated that human beings, be they men or women, were created from the same soul and were, therefore, equal to one another (Irwan, 2018). Later on, another verse—Omar 2014:102—reaffirms this by saying that women and men are equal partners (*The Quran, Omar 2014:102*,

1960). Yet the An-Nisaa chapter follows these ascertains with the claim that men are superior to women, which feels rather confusing. How could men and women be equal partners, after all, if men are superior to women?

It is because passages that seemingly contrast like this exist in the Qur'an that women's role in Islam cannot be very easily defined. This becomes doubly true when you consider the historical context in which Islam came to be. When Prophet Mohammed was given his revelation, women were living in rather poor conditions in that they did not have a lot of rights. Islam, however, made an effort to give them rights. For example, the Qur'an has a surah that officially gives them the right to own property and pursue their financial independence. At the same time, it forbade the killing of babies who were born as girls, modified marriage rules so that they were more beneficial to women, and modified divorce rules to protect women more (*Women in Islam*, n.d.).

When you consider things in this context, it becomes clear to see that Islam has strived to elevate the status of women and improve the conditions that they lived in. In a way, the role that Islam assigned to women in the 600s C.E. was more progressive than the roles they were assigned by other faiths and customs. Just because this role was more progressive, though, does not mean that they are progressive. Remember, men were still considered to be superior in Islam, and there is no denying the fact that the way certain surahs have been explained and interpreted have had important consequences on women's lives. Take the question of the hijab, for example. There are some women in the world who wear the hijab freely and willingly. There are others that are obligated and even forced to wear it, though. There are also women who have been and are still being barred from pursuing an education, career, and independence because of the limits that Islam—or maybe how it is being interpreted—places on them.

So, what is the role of women in Islam? How are women expected to be and act? If we want to understand women's true role in Islam, we must look at what the Qur'an says specifically about them, and the times Mohammed lived in. The Qur'an establishes that men and women are equal in creation, as we have seen. If you take a look at the story of Adam and Eve in the Qur'an, you find that blame for the original sin is not just ascribed to Eve here. Instead, Adam and Eve share the blame equally, as they are both tricked by the serpent. As an extension of that, the responsibility for their actions and the rewards or punishments they receive for them are completely equal as well. Aside from all that, the Qur'an specifically says that women and men (Al Khayat, 2003)

- are equal in their marital status and so are supposed to retain their surnames rather than have the woman take on her husband's surname.

- have an equal right to work and keep what they have rightfully earned.

- have a right to be paid equally for the same quality and amount of work.

- have equal rights to inheritance.

- have an equal right to pursue their education and are actually duty-bound to do so.

- are equally responsible for the family and household, which is why Mohammed at one point described wives and husbands as "shepherds," meaning it is not just a husband who is given this merit.

If all this is the case, though, why is Islam so misunderstood and misinterpreted? How is it Islam has come to be used as an oppressive tool in some cases? The roots of this situation can be traced back to women's role as mothers and their responsibility to bear children. Because of this responsibility, the Qur'an went on to state that while men and women have an equal right to work, work is a privilege for women, not an obligation. Some religious scholars argue this was stated to protect women, who could very easily die in childbirth and, thus, should not strain themselves.

Yet this is not the only way to interpret these words; hence some women being barred from the privilege of working. The Qur'an has also stated that men need to look after and take care of women. Again, some argue this surah exists to protect pregnant women, but it has been interpreted in a way that changes the power dynamics between men and women by some. This is the reason why women in Islam are sometimes forced into very constricting roles while others are not.

What can be concluded from all that is this: It is possible that Islam sought to establish genuine equality between women and men and to create a partnership between the sexes. This, however, has not come to pass, at least not for the most part. What has happened instead is a vast number of women have been obliged to take on very restrictive roles where they are defined by their obedience and submission to men. While this has not been the case for all women, it has been true for a great deal of them.

Part II:

Eastern Religions

Chapter 4:

Women in Hinduism

While a lot of people think Hinduism is polytheistic, it can technically be considered a monotheistic religion. A polytheistic religion is one that believes in multiple Gods. The reason Hinduism can be considered technically monotheistic is that it asserts that there is a main god, Brahma, that is the creator of all. Yet Hinduism does feature an array of deities in the form of gods and goddesses. These gods and goddesses are part of the universal soul that is Brahman, though. Hence, there is a sense of "oneness" among all the deities and all living beings really. This is the primary reason why Hinduism is technically monotheistic, even if it does have its own gods and goddesses.

The word "goddesses" is of note because there are a significant number of them in Hinduism. In fact, the feminine features quite heavily in Hinduism in some unexpected ways. When you look at the sacred texts of Hinduism, you find that women are often treated with a great deal of respect and reverence, hence the worshiping of goddesses. However, this does not change the fact that women's role in Hinduism is yet again one of support, especially in family and domestic life.

A Quick History of Hinduism

Hinduism is the oldest, still practiced religion in the entire world. Just as with other religions, Hinduism has its own sacred text, which is captured in scriptures known as the Vedas (Mark, 2020). There are some additional works, though, known as the *smritis*. The smritis contain stories about how to practice Hinduism, and these stories include famous epics such as the Ramayana.

All that being said, none of these scriptures, including the Vedas, can be considered the "word of God" in the way the Bible is, for example. What the Vedas say instead is that there is an undeniable truth to existence that is governed by Brahma, who is the Supreme Mind. This truth is ordered, structured, and rational, but more on that later. To go back to Hinduism's history, it is believed that the religion emerged in the 3rd century B.C.E. in the Indus Valley. It first arose among a tribe known as the Aryans. As people migrated away from the valley, they took their faith with them, and so the religion began spreading. The current iteration of Hinduism evolved from Brahmanism, a branch of Hinduism as it existed back then.

The Core Beliefs of Hinduism

So, what exactly do Hindus believe? First, Hinduism states that no matter what form you take and what you believe in, the only way to come to know God is to know yourself. Other key beliefs of the faith are that

- evil is born from ignorance of that which is good.

- discovering and learning about that which is good can negate evil.

- your purpose in life is to recognize good and pursue it.

- you will receive only evil if you do evil deeds and good for good deeds.

- the physical world is an illusion that we live in.

- you must fully participate in life by seeking three things: A good career and family life, the pleasure that is found in love and sexuality, and freedom and self-realization.

- though these three things are temporary pleasures, especially since the world is an illusion, the human soul derives enjoyment from them.

- the human soul used to be part of Brahman and is immortal.

- if you fail to attain self-realization in your life, your soul will reincarnate.

- if you succeeded in attaining self-realization, then your soul will rejoin Brahma upon your death.

The God that everyone eventually goes back to after attaining self-realization is Brahma, but what of the other deities? There are many deities in Hinduism, and goddesses are prominent among them. The characteristics associated with these goddesses and the responsibilities and stories attributed to them say a lot about the role women play in Hinduism. With that in mind, let's take a closer look at some of the chief goddesses in Hinduism to better understand women's role in their own religion, at least in the theoretical sense.

Goddesses in Hinduism

There are three main goddesses in Hinduism, and they are known as the Tridevi. These goddesses are Saraswati, Lakshmi, and Parvati (*Female Hindu deities–the Tridevi*, n.d.). Of these, Saraswati is the goddess of the arts, learning, and music. As Brahma's wife, she is probably the most powerful goddess out there and embodies the power of wisdom, pure thought, and knowledge. Her name literally means "the essence of the self."

Aside from all this, Saraswati is also a river goddess and a goddess of purity. Purity is, as we have seen, associated with women in many different religions. That it has, therefore, been associated with Saraswati is not a surprise. What may be a surprise is that qualities like wisdom, learning, and knowledge have been given to a female deity (Bhattacharyya, 2022). It may further be surprising that Saraswati is associated with the power of speech, especially after seeing how some religions ascribed silence to women. In Hinduism, speech is vital to invoke the powers of deities. The simple mantra "Om," for example, is the very sound of creation. That Saraswati is the goddess of speech, then, means that she is present whenever and wherever speech itself is.

Clearly, a lot of roles are ascribed to Saraswati. So important are these roles that not only is she currently the most worshiped goddess in Hinduism, but she's also more popularly worshiped than Brahma himself. Many universities in India, for example, bear her image on their walls, and schools have a specific day for celebrating her.

So, what does all this mean? Clearly, women have very elevated positions in Hinduism, right? In theory, yes. After all, qualities like wisdom, speech, knowledge, creativity, and learning are given to them through Saraswati. However, this theory does not always translate to reality the way it should, as we will see momentarily. For now, let's take a look at the second goddess in our Tridevi: Lakshmi.

Lakshmi is the goddess of wealth, royalty, beauty, luck, purity, and fertility (*Lakshmi*, n.d.). As you can see, some of these qualities are ones that are more typically associated with women. Purity and fertility have long been female qualities in a variety of religions and cultures, and Hinduism is no exception. Part of women's role is remaining chaste and pure and becoming wives and mothers, after all. Lakshmi represents a number of other qualities, too, such as marital fidelity, crop fertility, and spousal longevity. She has a very blissful marriage with Vishnu and is a devoted wife to him. As such, she can be taken as an exemplary wife role model for Hindu women.

Lakshmi's relationship with Vishnu is rather interesting, and thus has some interesting things to say to women about their roles in their own marriages. For instance, Lakshmi is very clearly subordinate to Vishnu and is obedient and utterly loyal to him as well. She is so loyal to her husband that when Vishnu reincarnates into the world as a mortal, Lakshmi puts her godhead to the side and chooses to reincarnate as a mortal right alongside her husband (Hughes, 2018). Of course, it takes a while for them to meet again, seeing as Lakshmi, now known as Sita, has to grow up from a baby into an adult once more but meet and remarry, and they eventually do.

After Rama and Sita wed, Rama is sadly banished, and Sita, again, does not let him go off to his banishment alone. Instead, she accompanies her husband along his long journey. Rama, in turn, puts Sita's well-being above all, even his own needs. Two things can be said based on all this. The first is that Lakshmi/Sita's story clearly tells women what their roles are: obedient, submissive, loving wives. The second is that Lakshmi/Sita and Vishnu/Rama's relationship does not just demonstrate how women should function in their roles as wives. It shows how husbands should function in their own roles and respond to and take care of their wives as well. In other words, it outlines how both sexes are supposed to comport themselves in their unique roles.

Finally, there is Parvati, who is female energy personified (*Parvati*, 2022). This female energy is called Shakti in Hinduism. Many see Parvati as the ultimate manifestation of the divine. She is very often depicted with her husband Shiva. Curiously enough, together, they are referred to as Ardhanarisvara, which means "the lord who is half woman." In this sense, Parvati and Shiva are two halves of a whole. As the female half of this whole, Parvati symbolizes things like domesticity, fertility, loyalty, and faithfulness. These are all familiar qualities that many different religions have attributed to women, as we have seen. However, Parvati has one specific quality that is assigned to her, and that is not usually assigned to women by other religions: female sexuality.

Assuming you are over 18 years old or have access to the internet, you have probably heard of the Kama Sutra. Well, you may be interested to know that this blush-worthy read can be considered Parvati's work. Well, more specifically, it can be considered Parvati and Shiva's work in that they created and enacted the various…poses in the book and then literally wrote them down. This was not Shiva's idea, by the way, though he certainly must have enjoyed the process. It was Parvati's. It was she who asked her husband to revive the Kama, and it was, thus, that they started to record their divinely inspired acts of desire, to put it in a poetic way.

When you look at Parvati, you see a woman who has very obviously embraced her sexuality and sexual appetite, something a lot of religions do not really allow, at least not blatantly. Parvati is allowed to do this because maintaining sexual desire is considered a domestic responsibility, for lack of a better term, and, thus, within the woman's purview. Women, then, are not only supposed to enact their desires but are encouraged to do so. It is quite literally one of their responsibilities, so long as they are married to the person they are making love to because there is purity and all that.

What do the Tridevi have to tell us about the role of women in Hinduism, then? For one, it is clear that this role is one where women are allowed to exercise their intelligence and make their voices heard. They are not expected to remain perpetually silent. This is as true of Parvati and Lakshmi as it is of Saraswati. Take a look at their stories, which are too vast to cover in their entirety here, and you will find that often these women give counsel to their husbands. There are times when they are incremental in changing their husband's minds and decisions. When Vishnu is about to give a particularly harsh punishment, it is Lakshmi who changes his mind. It is also her that acts as an intermediary between Vishnu, who is a rather taciturn fellow at times, and his followers to make sure the right requests are heard and honored.

At the same time, though, women are expected to mostly remain in the domestic sphere. Their primary roles are that of wife and mother, and in these roles, they are subservient, obedient, extremely loyal, caring, and faithful. In return, they are promised a relationship dynamic where they are respected, revered, and well-cared for. This is why the Vedas refer to women as dharma Patni, which means "she who promotes and protects the rightful conduct of life."

Contemporary Role of Women in Hinduism

Traditional Hinduism dictates that women are the supporters of their husbands, and their primary role is that of wife and mother, as we have said. However, the times are changing, and roles inevitably have to change with them. Women's role in Hinduism is no exception. This is why more and more modern Hindu women have been joining the workforce over the years (*Hinduism 101: Women and Hinduism*, 2017). Today, Hindu women have the right to hold a job and earn their own money, a right they did not really have in the past.

This change took place largely thanks to the many Hindu women who waged actual battles for it. Interestingly enough, many of these women used their own religion to make a case for change. One Hindu story they often turned to was the Bhagavad Gita, where Krishna, another very important male deity, very clearly states women are as capable and worthy of men as acquiring the freedom they desire.

While Hindu women have come a long way to expand their roles, it is undeniable that they still face a number of significant challenges. Many women are not accorded the respect they are promised in their own religion and yet are still expected to fulfill their traditional, domestic roles. As a most basic example, according to the Vedas, women are not forbidden from doing things like studying the Vedic texts. On the contrary, the Vedas have numerous stories depicting women pursuing just this freedom. Yet many women are barred from studying their religion in this way. This is just one small example of resistance women face when they try to change their societal roles, even when it is in ways that are theoretically permitted. Achieving this change fully and completely and in a practical sense is going to take more time and effort but will not be in any way unachievable.

Chapter 5:

Women in Buddhism

It seems controversial opinions and approaches to women exist in all walks—and religions—of life. Nowhere are these controversies more obvious than in Buddhism, though. That may seem a bold claim to make, especially considering how peaceful a religion Buddhism is, but it is not a baseless one. Buddhism is controversial when it comes to the topic of "women" because there are simply too many different attitudes directed toward them within the religion. Some of these attitudes are extremely misogynistic, to the point that they claim a woman cannot be considered a whole human being until she is reincarnated as a man (Paudel & Dong, 2017). Of course, there are far fewer misogynistic views and approaches to women and their role in Buddhism, too, as exemplified in Buddhist history and by the Buddha himself. Before we can go on discussing these different attitudes and what they signify about women's role in Buddhism, though, we have to first understand Buddhism's history and what it is all about.

A Quick History of Buddhism

The history of Buddhism begins with the Buddha. The story goes that Buddha was a prince. When he was born, a prophecy was made: If the young prince grew up never seeing any suffering of any kind, he would come to be a great king. If he grew up seeing suffering of any kind, he would come to be a great sage. His father obviously wanted him to be a king and never let him see anything bad growing up.

Buddha neither witnessed old age nor death nor illness and poverty. Things went on in this fashion until one day, he snuck away from the palace and encountered a poor man, a sick man, and a dead man. Confronted by suffering for the first time, he could not make sense of what he saw. Why did people have to suffer anyways? To find the answer to that question, he ran away from the palace for good. He meditated for 49 days beneath a Bo-tree, and when he rose, he had both the answer to his question and the solution to it. Said solution was, of course, Buddhism.

All this happened around the year 528 B.C.E. (Kohn, n.d.). Once Buddha had found his answer, he had to share it with others So, he took to traversing India on foot, spreading the word far and wide. His teachings attracted many pupils and eventually evolved into a full-fledged doctrine. His understanding of reality, which Buddhists call Dharma, was firmly established in the country by the year 483 B.C.E. Various monasteries had opened in the country too. It was only after the Buddha's death that his disciples put all his teachings down to writing. These teachings or sutras were eventually gathered together in Sutra Pitaka, Vinaya Pitaka, and Abhidhamma Pitaka. Taken together, these three are known as the Tripitaka and for the core of Buddhist scripture.

Following Buddha's death, Buddhism kept spreading across the country. Naturally, various different schools of thought and interpretations of it emerged as a result, which is partly the reason for those controversies and differing attitudes discussed earlier.

The Core Beliefs of Buddhism

Buddhism states that there are three universal truths and four noble truths. Together, these make the core beliefs of this faith. The three universal truths are (*Buddhism: Basic Beliefs*, 2019)

1. Everything in life is impermanent and therefore ever-changing.

2. A life that is about possessing different things and even people will not make you happy because everything is always changing.

3. The only unchanging thing on this earth is the soul, that is to say, the "self."

The four noble truths are

1. Human life is filled with suffering.

2. All suffering is caused by human greed.

3. Suffering is endless.

4. Suffering can be ended by following the Middle Way.

Following the Middle Way means spending your life without indulging in any luxuries and having too many indulgences. It also means leading the kind of life that is free from an overabundance of hardships and fasting. Following the Middle Way is the only way an individual can achieve Nirvana—not to be confused with the band. To achieve Nirvana and follow the Middle Way, you have to

- adopt a viewpoint that is based on the four noble truths

- have a compassionate rather than selfish attitude and values that support that attitude

- avoid telling lies, verbally abusing others, and gossip

- take selfless actions like helping others, taking care of the environment, and the like

- work in a useful, productive job that does not harm others in any way

- think helpful, good thoughts as much as possible and avoid negative thoughts

- practice mindfulness

- meditate to achieve a calm state of mind and Nirvana

In addition to all this, Buddhists have five precepts, that is to say, rules, that they all strive to follow, no matter which school of thought they adhere to. These five precepts are as follows:

1. Do not harm or kill any living beings, including animals.

2. Do not take anything that is not freely and willingly given to you.

3. Lead a good life.

4. Always be honest and do not speak unkindly of others.

5. Do not consume alcohol or take drugs.

All of these truths and precepts sound very good and sensible, do they not? If that is the case, though, then why do some schools of thought in Buddhism display a problematic attitude toward women? The main reason for this is that Buddhism has a patriarchal hierarchy and power dynamic. In some schools of thought, this structure has caused women to be associated with imperfection, temptation, and powerlessness. Traditional Buddhists associate women with the sensual—meaning those pleasures of the mortal realm that they are supposed to not indulge in. In other words, traditional Buddhists do not associate women and femininity with Dharma. Within this line of thinking, women are assigned one of two roles: a maternal source of pain for men or a lustful temptress that can damage the spiritual well-being of men and, especially, monks (Watts, 1987).

The lustful temptress role is most often symbolized by Mara and her daughters. In Buddhism, Mara is an evil temptress who does everything she possibly can do to make Buddha give up on his path and his enlightenment. When Buddha is meditating under the Bo-tree, Mara sends her three daughters to distract him and make him stray. These three daughters are Tanha, meaning desire, Raga, meaning lust, and

Arati, meaning aversion (Bourne, 2013). The three daughters' task was to distract Buddha, thereby breaking his concentration and keeping him from enlightenment. Despite their best efforts, though, Buddha never fell for their tricks. Instead, every time Mara sent her daughters to him, he just said, "Mara, I see you, and I am not afraid," and kept meditating until he reached enlightenment, or so the story goes.

On the one hand, the story of Mara and her daughters can be considered a great depiction of how we can overcome distractions and challenges that could keep us from our tasks. It can be considered a lesson on how to trust our inner wisdom and practice mindfulness and courage, and there are Buddhist schools of thought that embrace this interpretation. On the other hand, the story can be interpreted as a confirmation of women's role as temptresses and, thus, be used to condemn them. This is something other Buddhist schools of thought clearly do. This is clearly what is done in the Buddhist story called *The Tale of King Udayana of Valsa*, where the king describes women as a source of great suffering and talks about how desire should be destroyed (Mani, 2019). The king does not stop there, though. In the tale, he goes on to describe women as more detestable than dead snakes and dogs, which is certainly a haunting image.

What about mothers as sources of anguish, then? Some schools of thought consider mothers to be such sources of anguish because mothers represent a tie that binds men to their homes, which they eventually need to leave. In keeping with this line of thought, these schools of Buddhism believe that women cannot enter the spiritual or religious sphere, given how married they are to their domestic duties and realm. It is the merging of all such, let's be honest, misogynistic ideas that give rise to the belief women must be reincarnated as men to achieve dharma.

Luckily, not all Buddhist schools of thought are so misogynistic, and neither was the Buddha. While some Buddhists may say that women cannot see the Truth, Buddha disagreed. That is why he let women into the Order (Labde, 2021). Granted, he was hesitant to do so at first but realized the error in his thinking over time. So it was that women became fully ordained female equivalents of monks, known as *Bhikkhuni Sangas*. Bhikkhuni Sangas were incredibly well-learned preachers that, like other monks, aimed to teach others about Dharma.

One of the most famous Bhikkhuni Sangas is a woman called Dhammadinna (Ānandajoti, 2015). Dhammadinna was a married woman who became a Buddhist along with her husband. Upon discovering Buddhism, she decided she wanted to be a Bhikkhuni. While she managed to attain enlightenment, her husband did not, though he did rise to a certain degree. So it was that Dhammadinna became one of the many women that exceeded their husbands and even their own male teachers where spiritual education and enlightenment were concerned. In doing so, she demonstrated the fallacy of the misogynistic claims that try and still try to bar women from enlightenment.

Contrary to what some Buddhists think, then, real Buddhism holds that everyone, regardless of caste, origin, status, and, yes, sex has equal spiritual worth (Labde, 2021). It is a shame, then, that some schools of thought abjectly miss that fact, which is odd when you consider how Buddhist history features numerous very impressive women. Aside from Dhammadinna, for instance, there is Mahapajapati, who was Buddha's aunt (Watts, 1987). Mahapajapati was the first woman to ever be admitted into a Buddhist monastic order and, therefore, a trailblazer in every sense of the word.

That said, perhaps this attitude can be explained by considering the eight additional vows that Buddhist nuns were required to take when entering the Order. These vows essentially said that a nun, no matter how high her status may be, has to obey any monk as if they were her senior, even if his status was lower than hers. His maleness literally elevated his status over hers.

As for what was and is expected of Buddhist nuns in general, this changes slightly depending on which Buddhist tradition you are dealing with. In some Buddhist traditions, for example, female monks are required to shave their heads the same way male monks do. Hair has often been seen as a symbol of womanhood and femininity, but that is not why Buddhist nuns have to shave their heads. The real reason for this is that in Buddhism, ridding yourself of your hair is a symbolic renunciation of all things worldly, including fashion, beauty, and the ego (*Why do Buddhist Monks shave their heads?*, n.d.).

Known as tonsure, the practice of shaving your hair is a less gendered thing in this religion and has far more to do with the general values Buddhists seek to embrace and the way they try to adopt them. This is why in Buddhism, tonsure is part of the act of *Pabbajja*. Pabbajja is the official term for leaving your home and going forth to live out your life as either a Buddhist monk or a Buddhist nun, the same way that the Buddha did. All that being said, in most cases, Buddhist nuns are not required to shave their heads the way the monks are, but they are encouraged to do so as part of their spiritual practice. In the early days of Buddhism, the monastic community was almost exclusively male. In such a community, the practice of tonsure was seen as a way to distinguish monastics from laypeople. As Buddhism spread to different parts of the world, including Southeast Asia and East Asia, female monastic orders started emerging too. Thus, the practice of head shaving became more common among Buddhist women as well.

For women in the monastic tradition, head shaving is a symbolic act of renunciation and detachment from worldly concerns, something they do willingly. It is seen as a way of letting go of vanity and your attachment to your physical appearance. The idea here is to turn your focus instead to the pursuit of your spiritual development and enlightenment. Given that, some women choose to shave their heads as a sign of solidarity with the monastic community, even if they are not nuns or in an order of any kind. Such laywomen may choose to shave their heads for various reasons, including as a form of self-expression or as a way to show support for a particular cause or movement. In this sense, it can even become a tool of silent protest. However, tonsure is not a widespread practice, and neither is it typically associated with Buddhism as a whole.

Aside from shaving their heads, Buddhist nuns are also expected to wear simple robes as a sign of their commitment to a life of renunciation and spiritual practice. Again, the color of these robes changes depending on which order of Buddhism you are dealing with. Theravada nuns, for example, usually wear either light pink or white robes. Buddhist nuns in Nepal and Bhutan, on the other hand, usually wear maroon-colored robes (Rahman, 2023).

Contemporary Women's Roles in Buddhism

For all the positives that Buddhism has to offer, then, it is very clearly a patriarchal faith that has some very decided opinions on women and the role they should play. These opinions range from abjectly misogynistic to more subtle yet still restrictive. Given that, Buddhist women have their work cut out for them if they mean to change the role Buddhism ascribes to them. The good news is that women's efforts to change Buddhism's approach to their sex are very much in keeping with Buddhism itself.

Buddhism essentially came into being as a sramana movement, meaning that its purpose was to challenge the already-established religions of the time (Rinpoche, 2018). This is why Buddha himself faced a certain degree of opposition when he was working to spread the Truth. It is only to be expected, then, that women who seek to change Buddhism's view of themselves experience some degree of opposition as well. It is also only to be expected that they succeed in their mission, just as Yeshe Tsogyal has done.

Yeshe Tsogyal was a leading figure in Tibetan Buddhism. She was the foremost disciple of the legendary mystic Padmasambhava and an 8th-century Tantric master. In her quest for enlightenment, Yeshe Tsogyal has faced many challenges, including some that men seeking enlightenment would never face, including but not limited to the scorn of her fellow villagers, rape, and starvation. Despite these horrible challenges, Yeshe not only achieved enlightenment but became a revered figure among Tibetans. Today, women of the Nyingma School of Tibetan Buddhism are considered to be Yeshe's own emanations (Gayley, 2007).

The respect and welcome that Tibetan Buddhism gives to Yeshe and all other nuns that came after is due to the fact that this form of Tantric Buddhism affords women a unique place. Unlike other schools of thought in Tantric Buddhism, the feminine is revered for her wisdom, while the male is revered for his compassion. The idea here is that the two must go together for full enlightenment to be achieved. Of course, as with other religions, there is a strong link between women and motherhood in Tantric Buddhism too. However, in this school of thought, mothers are considered a source of love as opposed to anguish. Practitioners are, therefore, encouraged to meditate on maternal love and then extend that love to all living beings, no matter what their relationship with them is like. Given the connection between motherhood and womanhood, Tibetan Buddhism holds forth that women's role in the world is to curb people's excesses and give love to all. It ascertains that it is women, not men, who are responsible for and capable of making a better world for all (*Women in Tibetan Buddhism*, 2021).

Chapter 6:

Women in Taoism

Unlike the grand majority of the religions we have seen so far, Taoism has a special connection with women and the feminine. It can even be said that the feminine is a vital part of Taoism, seeing as it harbors core concepts such as the Mysterious Feminine, which is where all of creation and space itself came from. Before we can discuss all this and women's role in Taoism in detail, though, we must first understand what Taoism is. Otherwise, we risk misunderstanding the concepts that formulate this philosophy, way of life, and religion and, therefore, how it affects women and their unique roles in the world.

A Quick History of Taoism

Taoism—sometimes written as Daoism—is a philosophy that emerged in Ancient China around the year 500 B.C.E. It was created by Lao Tzu, who may or may not have actually existed; we are not entirely sure. If he did exist, though, he literally wrote the book on Taoism (*Taoism*, 2023). Said book is known as the *Tao Te Ching*, which means "The Way of the Power." Of course, *Tao Te Ching* is not filled with Lao Tzu's sayings but rather is an accumulation of sayings that were made by many other authors.

Taoism is based on the idea that all living beings, humans and animals alike, must live in balance with the universe, otherwise known as the Tao. Taoism was the main religion of the Tang Dynasty in China, which reigned over the country in the 8th century. It co-existed with other philosophies and religions of the time, like Buddhism and Confucianism.

Taoism was widely practiced in China until 1949 when the Communists took over the country. At that point, Taoism was banned, right alongside Confucianism and Buddhism. So it was that Taoism declined significantly in China. Today, the religion is mostly practiced in Taiwan, although it has been having a Chinese resurgence of late.

The Core Beliefs of Taoism

Taoism is all about living in harmony with the universe and the other beings that populate it, as you have seen. This is because Taoism believes that the human spirit will join the universe upon the death of the body. That means that the human body is mortal while the human spirit is not. Taoist thoughts, beliefs, and actions are guided by the teachings of the *Tao Te Ching*.

"Tao" itself can be seen as a way of perceiving and understanding the universe. All living beings live in harmony with the universe and the energy that makes up the universe. This energy is not a "God," however, because Taoism does not have a God the way other religions like Judaism does. There are Gods in Taoism that accompany certain beliefs, but more often than not, they come from regional cultures in China that Taoism has become a part of.

The core idea of Taoism is that life is a balancing act between "yin" and "yang." Yin and yang are matching but opposing pairs. Light and dark are examples of yin and yang, for instance. So are hot and cold, fast and slow, and feminine and masculine. In Taoism, the feminine is yin, and the masculine is yang.

Women in Taoism

Since Taoism is about balance and since "the feminine" is considered to be yin, which needs to be in balance with yang, femininity and women are an integral part of Taoism. As mentioned before, Taoists believe that all creation came from the Mysterious Feminine (NÍ G, n.d.). Taoists also believe that "Tao" itself is a feminine concept and Yin.

The reason the feminine is considered to be yin is that the typical qualities of yin are listening, surrendering, being receptive, and having a natural flow. These qualities are, therefore, ascribed to women too. Women are, thus, thought to be soft rather than hard, which does not mean that women are considered to be weak. The *Tao Te Ching* expressly says, "softness overcomes hardness," after all, like water flowing around a large rock (Tse, 2007).

Since both Tao and the feminine are yin, Taoists believe that women are more easily able to connect with Tao and therefore are better able to draw from forces of nature, Earth, and the heavens. As such, women are able to reach enlightenment quicker than men can. This is why women were thought of and treated as the holders of Taoist tradition in the Tang dynasty. It was women who taught others Taoist practices, as well as things like healing practices and magic. It was also women who founded actual schools to teach as many people as humanly possible.

One of the most important aspects of Taoism is that, unlike a lot of religions, it never repressed female sexuality. On the contrary, it greatly encouraged it. In fact, ancient Taoists are considered to be the first sexologists in history. The work they did in sexuality resulted in no less than an actual sexual liberation movement that rivals the sexual liberation movements of the 60s, and this was around the year 500 B.C.E.! A look at the massively detailed reports that early Taoists wrote on the female sexual response is enough to confirm as much. This makes sense when you think about it. I mean, why would you try to repress something rather than seek to understand it more and embrace it if you truly believe it is a natural part of the world that exists in balance with male sexuality?

The amount of time and effort ancient Taoists devoted to studying female sexuality may seem excessive to some. It starts making a lot more sense, though, when you recall that Taoists considered sexual energy to be the strongest form of energy in the world. Sexuality and sexual energy are so important in Taoism that Tang Dynasty emperors actually had numerous sexual advisors, and often a significant number of them were women. Taoism put special emphasis on female satisfaction during intercourse, which is something more modern men should probably take note of. This was so important, in fact, that men who were newly initiated into Taoism were actually given lessons on how to delay ejaculation. Their masters made a point to inform them that women had inexhaustible, near-infinite desire. They, therefore, advised their pupils to try to give a "thousand loving thrusts" (NÍ G, n.d.).

Women's Role in Taoism

So, what does all this mean for women's role in Taoism? Does it make Taoism a religion that has achieved complete or at least near complete gender equality? Hardly. It is true that, at its core, Taoism values duality and recognizes that both femininity and masculinity are necessary forces of nature and life. However, this belief does not translate into practical equality. Taoism specifically emphasizes the role of women as mothers and ascribes nurturing characteristics to them (Reninger, 2019). Furthermore, it has a very strict, patriarchal hierarchy, even if women are expected to teach others of Taoism.

While women are expected and allowed to teach these concepts to, say, their children, and though women could become advisors on Taoist sexuality to emperors, very few women were allowed to become priests. This is because someone wanting to become a priest needed an education, and women were too often barred from receiving an education. There were exceptions, of course, and one of these rare exceptions was a woman called Sun Bu-Er. Originally named Sun Fuchun, Sun Bu-Er was born in 1119 (Xuan Yun, n.d.). Unlike a lot of her contemporaries, she was lucky enough to receive an education, which is one of the benefits of being born into a wealthy family.

At first, Sun Bu-Er's life followed the trajectory of a typical woman of her time. She married a man named Ma Yu and had three sons with him. She tended to her home and was seemingly content. Then, at 51 years old, she met Wang Chongyang a Taoist master. Thus, she became enamored, not with Master Chongyang but with Taoism itself, as did her husband, Ma Yu. Ma Yu fell so in love with the faith, in fact, that he decided to become a disciple of the faith. The problem was this: Disciples of Taoism needed to take vows of celibacy. Ma Yu, however, was married. So, how did they solve this problem? By getting a divorce, of course!

Originally, Sun Bu-Er was not going to follow in her now ex-husband's example, especially since becoming a disciple would require relinquishing the financial security and social status she held. It would also mean cutting off contact with her friends and family, including her children. Given the steep price Sun Bu-Er would have had to pay, it is understandable that she would not wish to become a disciple. Yet it seems she eventually changed her mind because just two years later, Sun Bu-Er had become a disciple of Master Yang as well.

Master Yang's disciples would, in time, come to be known as the Seven Perfected, and Sun Bu-Er, was the only female member of the Seven Perfected. As one of the group, she studied for years under Master Yang's guidance and, upon his death, traveled to Shaanxi Province, despite how perilous a journey this was for a woman alone. It was in this province that she at last attained complete oneness with the Tao through solitary meditation. After that, she traveled to a cave hermitage, where she lived out the rest of her days and, as the story goes, threw rocks at the men passing by to ward off temptation. That is certainly one way of driving away unwanted attention, I suppose.

At the cave hermitage, Sun Bu-Er acquired and guided disciples of her own. In 1182, she foresaw her own death. Upon sensing what was to come, she gathered all her disciples around her, recited a poem to them, and passed away before their eyes. As her spirit ascended to the heavens, her ex-husband, who was miles and miles away at the time, actually witnessed her journey. He celebrated her ascension by tearing off his clothes and dancing in her honor, which is an interesting response to give to your ex-wife's passing, to say the least.

The very interesting thing about Sun Bu-Er is not that she was one of the few female Taoist priests of her time. It is that she became celebrated enough for entire monasteries and temples to be opened in her honor. These monasteries and temples eventually came to be home to some 20,000 priests, 6,000 of whom were women. While that does not even make up half of the total number of priests, it is still a marked rise in female priests, something that can easily be attributed to her reputation and accomplishments.

Sun Bu-Er's journey, then, is a great example of how one exception can change the destiny and roles of the women of the future. This is likely something a lot of women desired, considering the rather restrictive role Taoism ascribed to women, despite all its talk of balance and harmony. In Taoism, women were given a very specific position in society, as well as within their families. This position was one of subservience, as always. In Taoism, women were to submit first to their fathers, then to their husbands. Should a woman's husband die, she needed to submit to her son instead!

That being said, women still occupied some significant roles in Taoism. Though they seldom became priests, they could become oracles and mediums and thus commune with the spirits (Reninger, 2019). Of course, just because few women could become priests in the past does not mean that that is still the case. You see, Taoism was able to make a resurgence in the 20th century thanks, in large part, to women. It was they that took up and took to spreading the religion once more. It was also women that started pursuing a spiritual education in Taoism. Thanks to their efforts, a third of all Taoist priests are now women, and that figure is still on the rise. This is something that would have been unfathomable a couple of hundred years ago.

Chapter 7:

Women in Confucianism

Another religious philosophy to emerge in Ancient China was Confucianism. Like Taoism, Confucianism began as a philosophy of sorts and later took on heavy, religious undertones (*Taoism and Confucianism—ancient philosophies*, n.d.). Created by Confucius in the 6th century B.C.E., Confucianism existed side-by-side in ancient China. While there were and are some important similarities between the two, Confucianism imposed far stricter gender roles and rules to live by on women than Taoism did. This difference between the two religions can partly be attributed to the fact that Confucianism seems to deal with social matters a whole lot more than Taoism does. While they harbor certain similar beliefs on the nature of man and the universe itself, they did differ on some important points.

A Quick History of Confucianism

So, how is it that two religions that emerged around the same time, in the same country no less, ended up being more different than they were similar? To comprehend this, we must first take a look at how Confucianism developed. Confucianism was created by the philosopher and teacher Confucius, who lived from the year 551 B.C.E. to 479 B.C.E. When Confucianism first came into being, it did so as a life philosophy rather than a religion. Over the years, it evolved to take more religious undertones.

Today, it is considered a religious philosophy, though there are people who disagree with this assessment and see it more as a philosophy than a religion. These people, however, miss the fact that Confucianism was built on some earlier religious traditions of ancient China. They also forget the fact that while Confucianism does not put forth a god to believe in, its followers do worship Confucius' spirit (Appleton & Willis, 2022). They even forget or perhaps do not know about the existence of the many temples that have been built for Confucianism across the centuries. These temples are important institutions where various civic rituals take place, and rituals are a vital part of any religion, as we all know.

Following its inception, Confucianism became one of the leading and most influential belief systems in ancient China. Emperor Wu-ti of the Han Dynasty, for instance, who ruled over China between the years 141 and 87 B.C.E. decreed Confucianism as the empire's official ideology. Following this declaration, numerous Confucianist schools were opened across the country, and these schools instructed their pupils in Confucianism ethics. The influence of Confucianism, thus, spread far and wide and would continue to be felt in China and beyond for many years to come. During the Song Dynasty, which reigned over China between the years 960 and 1270 CE, elements of Confucianism, Taoism, and Buddhism seemed to meld together since all three existed in the same region in the same years. This gave rise to a belief system ideology known as Neo-Confucianism.

Neo-Confucianism came to an end in the Qing Dynasty, and Confucianism resumed its power in its original form between the years 1644 and 1912, while the Qing Dynasty was in power. Suffice it to say, then, that Confucianism has long influenced China's beliefs, way of life, society, and, therefore, the role that women were allowed to play in it.

The Core Beliefs of Confucianism

The Confucian canon consists of not one single holy book but rather of nine key texts. These texts are known as the Four Books (*shi shu*) and the Five Classics (*wujing*), respectively (Wilson, 2010). The four works that make up the Four Books are

- the Analects

- the Great Learning

- the Doctrine of the Mean

- Mencius

The Analects are a collection of aphorisms said by and anecdotes featuring Confucius himself. These aphorisms and anecdotes were not written by Confucius but rather by his disciples after his death. In essence, they embody the core values of Confucius ideology and traditions, which are morality, learning, filial piety, and ritual decorum (Watson, 2007). Of these, learning is the first step people need to take in order to devote themselves to the Way (Wilson, 2010).

The Great Learning, meanwhile, is a sort of guidebook on self-development and self-cultivation. The key to these two things is investigation and learning, or so the book says, and it is only through these acts that a person can bring their principles (their li) and psychophysical aspects (their qi) in line with one another.

The Doctrine of the Mean is said to be written by Confucius' grandson Zisi and focuses on the means by which an individual can bring balance to their life. The idea presented here is that you always have to act according to what's right and natural if you want to achieve balance and harmony, even if this is hard to do for most people. The Doctrine of the Mean further emphasizes that governance of all things, from the actual government to the family, rests on the shoulders of men, not women, who are the leaders needed to maintain balance.

Lastly, there is *Mencius*, which is a collection of conversations that take place between Confucius and another philosopher named Mencius. Mencius puts forth the idea that all human beings are born inherently good and moral but need to learn to cultivate those traits as they grow up and grow older.

As you might have guessed from the nature of these texts, the core idea behind Confucianism is the importance of being of good moral character. A good moral character is something that can affect the world around you and allow you to achieve perfect harmony with the cosmos (Appleton & Willis, 2022). A ruler who is of perfect moral character, for example, will have an utterly peaceful and benevolent reign. In keeping with that line of logic, Confucianism attributes natural disasters such as earthquakes or tsunamis to people's immoral choices and behaviors. Morality, then, is essential if humanity wants to avoid such drastic consequences.

Confucianism dictates that achieving morality is only possible through humility, respect, and altruism. While all human beings are born inherently good, they must cultivate that goodness through actions that display these qualities, and they must educate themselves on what virtuous behavior truly is and looks like. The rituals that Confucianism has its practitioners and believers partake in are meant to instruct them on what genuine, respectful attitudes and a true sense of community look like.

Another core concept in Confucianism, which is very important with respect to women's role in it, is filial piety. Otherwise known as devotion to family, this translates to absolute submission to parents and things like ancestor worship. In Confucius society, the family unit is seen as the most important unit of society. By being devoted to your family, then, you can actually strengthen the society that you are a part of, or so the idea goes.

Women in Confucianism

Filial piety, coupled with the long-standing ideas regarding women's place in the domestic sphere, has led to Confucianism developing some very concrete ideas about women's role in their families and societies. These ideas are very clearly expressed in didactic texts that were written specifically for women, such as the *Four Books for Women* and biographies of exemplary women. The existence of such texts created an interesting dichotomy in Confucianism. On the one hand, these texts clearly emphasized women's place in the home and primary role as mothers and wives. On the other hand, they fostered women's learning, leadership, and even authorship in a setting where literacy was traditionally reserved for men alone (Rosenlee, 2023). In an interesting turn of events then, Confucianism gave women an unexpected opportunity for education, even if what source material they were expected to learn was very specific.

In the Confucius belief system, the family took priority, and this meant some very specific things for women. For one, it meant that their womanhood depended on their ability to get married and integrate into their husbands' families. Once married, women were expected to obey their husbands, the head of the household, seeing as men were the expected leaders in all things. They were tasked with caring for their husbands and families, performing domestic duties, and giving birth to and raising kids. Ideally, they were expected to give birth to boys because male heirs were preferable as a general rule. Before marriage, they were expected to obey their parents' authority, especially that of their fathers, in all things. They had to be pure and virginal before marriage.

For all its rigidity where women's role is concerned, though, Confucianism valued women in a similar way that Taoism did in that it understood the feminine and masculine need to be balanced in the world. Hence, Confucianism harbored the concept of yin and yang as well, which is just one thing it has in common with Taoism. This is likely part of the reason why Confucianists referred to the rulers of ancient China as "the fathers and mothers of the people." The parental parity that the title brings with it is interesting to make note of. Another interesting thing about Confucianism is that, unlike a lot of religions, philosophies, and ideologies, it does not describe women as morally, characteristically, intellectually, or otherwise inferior to men in any way. On the contrary, Confucian texts seem to afford women the same level of intelligence, morality, and, therefore, respect that it affords to men. A quick look at how women are described in, say, *Exemplary Women's Biographies*, which was written in 18 B.C.E. by Liu Xiang is enough to prove as much.

It can honestly be said that women are not considered inferior in nature to men in Confucianism. Why are women confined to the domestic sphere, then? This has to do with the already existing hierarchical relationship between wives and husbands. In ancient China, women were expected to follow the men's lead, a concept that Confucianism naturally embraced. Like in many other patriarchal religions and cultures, women are subservient to men in their roles, where Confucianism is concerned.

Part III:

Women in Indigenous Religions

Chapter 8:

Women in Indigenous African

Religions

Describing the role of women in indigenous African religions is a somewhat difficult undertaking. This is because the continent of Africa is home to a very wide array of traditional beliefs. As such, covering all of them in the span of a single chapter is nearly impossible to accomplish. However, identifying the main commonalities of these religions is certainly possible. For all their differences, traditional African religions are united in three things: They are all animistic, they all put specific emphasis on ancestry worship, and they all define women's role in family, society, and life in very specific ways. We will begin examining women's role in indigenous African religions by taking a look at these unifying factors. Since there are too many belief systems to choose from, we will focus on just two traditional African religions to draw examples. These religions will be the Yoruba and Igbo cultures, both of which are indigenous to Nigeria.

The Commonalities of Traditional African Religions

Traditional African religions are generational, meaning they have been handed down from parents to children for generations. The beliefs, customs, and traditions making up these religions have, therefore, been going on for centuries and still exist today. This very fact makes traditional African religions more dynamic than many other kinds of faith. Unlike Christianity, for example, these religions constantly respond and react to the changes that come with modernity and time. Far from being stagnant, they adapt to modernity as necessary while still holding on to their roots. There is a simple reason traditional African religions are able to do this: They are less traditions of faith than they are traditions that are lived. Put another way, traditional African religions have far less to do with theory and doctrine and far more to do with lived practices, customs, and ceremonies (Olupona, 2014).

So, what exactly are the common points of all these traditional African religions? First, traditional African religions all believe in the existence of one superior creator, God, who resides in the heavens (*Africa traditional religious system*, 2000). That is not to say they necessarily believe in the existence of heaven, but rather in a different plane of reality than the one we live in. Second, traditional African religions are polytheistic. While they all have a creator, a God of some sort, they have other gods and goddesses in their pantheon. They also have room for many supernatural beings and spirits.

The belief in spirits is closely tied to ancestor worship in traditional African religions. The religions hold that the spirits of those that pass on do not wholly disappear. Rather, they can be communicated with, and these spirits, when malicious, can even harm others. In African cultures, there are specific individuals—both men and women—who are able to communicate with these spirits. Such individuals are known as shamans, medicine men and women, diviners, and seers. They use objects found in nature, along with charms, amulets, and magic, to communicate with these spirits or divine things. They also make use of wild plants and animal components to prepare medicine and magic. They possess the power to transmit mysterious abilities through spiritual means or certain objects. Of course, such mystical powers can be used both for enacting good deeds and for harming others.

Traditional African religions, then, can be said to be inherently shamanistic and animistic. They also place great value on both ancestors and spirits. So much so that many African religions' understanding of destiny is deeply tied to their understanding of the spirit world. The spirit world is made up of two different kinds of spirits: human spirits and nonhuman ones. These spirits reside in an array of different places, like in baobab trees, rocks, rivers, and more. This is one way in which the animistic core of traditional African religions is manifested. There are both bad and good spirits, just as those who can use mystical powers for evil and good purposes.

As for which gods and goddesses African religions believe in, this depends entirely on which African tribe and culture you are dealing with. Take the Igbo belief system, which is known as Odinani, for instance, practiced by the Igbo people of West Africa. Igbo people believe in a creator god called Chukwu or Chineke (The Editors of Encyclopaedia Britannica, 2019). He is the source from which everything, including the other deities that Igbo people believe in, came from. It is Chukwu who assigned these deities their various roles too.

Aside from Chukwu, there is Ala, the earth goddess, who is the goddess of fertility, creativity, and morality as well (Ojukutu-Macauley, 2021). Said to be the mother of all things, Ala is present at both the very beginning of life and the very end of life. While she's not the creator of the earth, she's considered to be the highest deity among all gods and goddesses that the Igbo believe in. This has had a very interesting effect on Odinani and has resulted in the Igbo culture putting women ahead of men.

The Role of Women in Odinani

The reason Odinani puts women ahead of men has to do with Ala's position among the deities. Think about it: that she is present at both the beginning and very end of life means she presides over life and death. This means that she's there both when babies are born and when planted crops begin yielding their fruit. It means that she is there when someone passes away and when a flower withers or a harvest field remains empty. Not only is Ala present for all these things, but, being the goddess of morality, she's also in charge of managing Igbo law, which is known as Omanala. An individual who commits a crime, say theft, is, therefore, said to have directly insulted Ala herself. It is said that Ala punishes such people by sending an army of ants after them. If you have ever been bitten by a fire ant, you know exactly how painful that can be and can probably imagine how horrid dealing with an army of them would be too.

Igbo people celebrate Ala with the arrival of spring. They give her offerings when it is planting season, as well as when it is time for plants to yield their fruit and for harvesting. Villages have a shrine devoted to Ala at their very core. Offerings are often left at these shrines on a daily basis, but especially during important celebrations. One of the best ways of paying tribute to Ala is to light candles in her honor in the morning to celebrate the arrival of spring. It is believed that doing this is the best way to receive Ala's blessing of fertility and creativity.

That is all well and good, but what does it mean for Igbo culture to put women ahead of men? Does it mean men and women were equal within this belief system? Not really. However, it does mean that Igbo women are allowed to play a larger part in both their families and the societies they live in as decision-makers (Egbo, 2021). In the past, women's primary role within Igbo society was that of an honorable and pure wife for their husbands. That meant adopting a more submissive role within the house, as well as taking on domestic duties, child-raising responsibility, and the like. At the same time, however, women were actually made part of the governing systems of their societies. In Igbo culture, there are two community entities responsible for governance: *Um Ikom* and *Umu Inyom*. Um Ikom is made up of men, whereas Umu

Inyon is made up of all women. All of these women are married, and the head of Um Inyon is the oldest married wife.

So, what exactly does Umu Inyon have a say in? Umu Inyon typically looks at cases of child abuse, domestic abuse perpetuated against women, ill-treatment of wives by their husbands, and the like. Upon hearing these cases, it is the women of Umu Inyon that metes out the appropriate punishment for them. Like Ala, then, it can be said that the rules of morality and safeguarding of their sex and children were entrusted to them. So, while women's roles veered to the traditional in many regards in Igbo society, it also broke the mold in others.

Another way Igbo women broke the mold can be seen in some of the rules concerning their marriage. Igbo women were actually allowed to marry other women. These same-sex marriages were typically a privilege afforded to women of exceptional standing within society or to women who had passed through menopause (Egbo, 2021). They proved a significant way for women to obtain the same societal privileges afforded to men, sometimes putting them on the same status as their village elders. It also was a way for women to obtain greater sexual freedom. Some heterosexual women would marry other women so that they could pursue relationships with their male love interests while creating an environment of financial security for themselves. Within Igbo society, these men were referred to as "sperm donors," allowing these women in same-sex marriages to have kids to raise them without having to find a husband (Aliyu, 2018). Any children that these women then bore would take on the surnames of the women they had married, and yes, this was a widely accepted cultural practice in Igboland.

What all this tells us about women in the Igbo belief system is that while they were expected to fulfill more domestic roles, they had far greater freedom than most of their contemporaries around the world. Not only did their role allow them to take leadership positions within their societies once they had met their marital requirements, but it also afforded them a great deal of sexual freedom. Of course, the Igbo belief system was not the only traditional African religion to afford such things to women. Take the Yoruba people, for instance. Though they did not hold to the same beliefs that the Igbo people did, they did treat women in similar ways in some regards. The Yoruba belief system, which is known as Isese, also allowed women to enter into same-sex marriages, for instance, and was, in fact, one of the many African religions to permit this.

The General Beliefs of Isese

Before diving into women's role in *Isese*, let's quickly cover what Isese is all about. Isese is the core belief system of the Yoruba people, which make up about a fifth of Nigeria's population (Gordon, 2003). The supreme creator god of Isese is Orudumale or Olorun (Dopamu, 1999). He's the absolute ruler over all the other deities, who are, in fact, his offspring. These deities are known as the *orishas*. The orishas are something of an intermediary between Olorun and humans (Wigington, 2019). At times they work on human beings' behalf. At others, they work against them. Like the gods and goddesses of Ancient Greece, they behave a lot like human beings.

Aside from the orishas, there is also the *Ajogun*. The Ajogun are negative forces in the world, which cause misfortunes like illnesses. Most things in life can be explained as the doings of the orishas and Ajogun, then.

According to Isese, all deities and human beings contain the same life force within them. This life force is known as *Ashe*, and it is found in all natural beings as well. When a person dies, they rejoin the divine creator, who is the source that Ashe comes from.

Isese is one of the most complicated religions in the world, in that it features some 6,000 gods and goddesses. Of these, one of the most important is Oya. She is the goddess of water, fertility, and acts of creation. When a Yoruba woman wishes to get pregnant, she is to make an offering of food or drink to Oya (*Deities of the Yoruba*, n.d.). While Oya can be quite benevolent, she's also a very mischievous goddess, which is a characteristic that most polytheistic religions attribute to male gods as opposed to female goddesses. Think Loki from Norse Mythology, for instance. Oya's mischievousness comes from her association with nature. The image of "Mother Nature" seems to be a persistent one in nearly every culture, given the Earth's nurturing, crop-growing abilities. The Yoruba have taken this association a step further where Oya is concerned, though. As such, they have taken things like winds strong enough to break trees and destroy croplands and attribute them to Oya's mischievousness.

The Role of Yoruba Women

Yoruba women hold an important place in Isese rituals and traditions. At the same time, they have been assigned the typical "mother and wife" role that most religions seem to have given women. This role naturally comes with certain expectations. For example, women are expected to be virgins before marriage, and their virginity is intimately tied to their honor and that of their family. A woman who is not a virgin when she gets married is believed to bring dishonor to herself and her family (Familusi, 2012). To make sure that is not the case, tradition dictates that members of a bride and bridegroom's families spend the night sleeping in front of the newlywed couple's bedroom so that they can hear the cry of pain the bride will let out on losing her virginity.

Following her marriage, a woman is expected to be faithful to her husband, though such expectations can't be said to be placed on her husband. After all, not only is a Yoruba woman expected to remain calm should she find out her husband had an extramarital affair, but she's also expected to be accepting of the other five wives he is allowed to have. It goes without saying that women are not allowed to have six husbands.

Women are further expected to be paragons of morality in the Yoruba culture and belief system. Since their primary role is that of mother and wife, they are often considered the agents of moral ineptitude and, thus, blamed for their children's bad behavior if and when they act out.

Clearly, Yoruba women are expected to fit into more confining roles that follow very stringent rules. Aside from their family-oriented roles, they have some specific roles and responsibilities in religious rituals and customs, as mentioned before, though they are exempted from these responsibilities when they are on their cycle (Wigington, 2019). Traditionally, Yoruba women have taken on the role of priestesses. While the religion and culture are male dominated, it is interesting that it makes enough room for women to lead religious practices, unlike some other belief systems. Perhaps this can be tied back to the Yoruba people's understanding of reincarnation. Yoruba people believe in reincarnation. They believe everyone possesses a soul, and that soul can be reborn in either a male or female body, regardless of what gender they were in their previous life. This belief is reflected in traditional Yoruba names like "Yetunde," which means mother returns.

Women's Role in Traditional African Religions

The continent of Africa is home to between 1,000 and 2,000 languages and around 3,000 tribes. That equals a maddening number of different religions and belief systems, whichever way you cut it. Discussing women's role in all these religions is impossible to do, at least in the span of this chapter. However, arriving at certain conclusions about this role, based on the two examples we have looked at and the commonalities between these various religions we have explored, is more than possible. The primary conclusion we can arrive at is that women usually play mother, wife, and caregiver roles in traditional African religions. When looking at the mythology that these different religions feature, women are seen as "mothers of mankind," and sources of fertility and progeny become obvious (Okunade, 2022).

One interesting commonality between vastly different African traditional religions is that women often play important ritualistic roles in the practice of their faith. In some communities, like the Yoruba and Igbo, women are allowed to become priestesses. They very frequently become midwives and medicine women who use natural remedies to help people. Recent findings, for instance, have shown that African women had been performing successful c-sections for hundreds of years before the practice was "invented" in Europe (Jones & Chamberlin, 2023). Most of these medicine women specialized in children's and women's health. Essentially, they became their own family doctors, as they were expected to take care of the basic medical needs of their family—something that supposedly falls under the definition of "mother, wife, and caregiver" (Zimoň, 2006).

Chapter 9:

Women in Native American

Religions

How about Native American women, then? As with traditional African religions, taking a comprehensive look at all the different Native American religions out there and examining women's role in them is not possible to do in the span of a single chapter. There are a total of 574 different indigenous tribes in the United States that are recognized by the federal government (*Federally recognized Indian tribes*, n.d.). What is possible to do is to consider the general commonalities in different Native American religions, take a look at some examples, and try to observe women's general role in these religions, cultures, and communities. This is slightly challenging to do because of the overarching influence that Western cultures and religions have had on Native American tribes and their cultures. Genocide and oppression tend to have that effect, sadly. Nonetheless, there are resources and studies we can turn to to understand these cultures and beliefs and the role that women play in them to the best of our abilities.

The Commonalities of Native American Religions

There are as many different Native American belief systems as there are Native American tribes in the United States. No two belief systems are the same. However, these belief systems do share some commonalities. For starters, Native American faiths are oral traditions, not written ones. They do not come with holy books the way Abrahamic Religions or religions like Hinduism do. Instead, these faiths are passed down through the generations and contain entire cosmologies of their own. These cosmologies all feature a creation myth of some sort, other deities, spirits, supernatural entities, and mythical creatures that all these figures take part in (Heyrman, n.d.).

One major commonality in all Native religions is that they believe in a "Master Spirit," or omnipotent and omniscient creator God of some sort. The name, form, gender, or genderlessness of this god or being changes from religion to religion. This Master Spirit, otherwise known as the Great Spirit, was thought to be anthropomorphic, meaning that it had human features and characteristics. In most Native American folklore, it was responsible for the creation of the Earth and the Universe and, at times, interfered with human lives and events. Another important commonality is that Native religions believe in the immortality of the soul, as well as in the existence of an afterlife for that soul. This afterlife typically is one where the human soul rejoins the great spirit.

What essentially shaped these different Native beliefs is that Native tribes believed they could influence the supernatural forces at work by shaping and directing the natural and social factors under their control. So it was that prayers and rituals to appease various gods, spirits, and other entities were born. The same goes for offerings and sacrifices made to these beings. When something large was needed for the entirety of a village or tribe, the people started to come together under the guidance of priests, priestesses, or shamans who would be able to see visions that could help them in their endeavors.

Native American religions, then, were shamanistic and placed great significance on nature and natural events. As such, they respected nature and the beings that populated the natural world greatly. This makes a lot of sense, considering the nomadic lifestyle that Native American tribes led. Take the Inuit people, for example. Living in a rather frigid environment in Alaska, the survival of the Inuit people has largely been dependent on fishing and hunting. As a result, the Inuit treat nature with an immense amount of respect (*The Inuit people*, n.d.).

Inuit people believe that every animal possesses a soul, known as the *inua* (*Inuit religious traditions*, n.d.). This is what is known as animism. They further believe that things like lakes and mountains, even the moon have their own inua. Since a being with a soul deserves respect, the Inuit take care to offer it to animals, even when hunting them. When the Inuit hunted seals, for example, they would offer the animal they had caught a drink of water. They believed that upon receiving this kind welcome, the caught seal would have a drink of water, and then its soul would vacate its body, thus returning to the ocean. Here, the seal would be reborn again, and it would tell its kind of the gracious treatment it had received. It would tell its kind, the belief went, to allow themselves to be hunted. This kind of thing was not just done with seals but with every animal that was hunted. Generally speaking, such behavior was a way of showing the hunted animal's inua respect.

The Role of Inuit Women

The respect shown to animals is not specific to the Inuit. It is something that all Native tribes possess. One other significant commonality between Inuit beliefs and other Native American beliefs is seen in the role and treatment of women. Since Inuit people believe that all things, from animals to rivers, have their own inua, they maintain that it is possible to communicate with these spirits. When a tribe or individual wants to communicate with a specific spirit or inua, they turn to a shaman. Shamans are revered in Inuit culture and might be the most important individual in their community.

Able to influence the decisions that tribal councils make, shamans can please or appease spirits and, thus, obtain the things the tribe needs, like good rainfall for the year, for instance. In Inuit culture, female shamans are preferred to male shamans. This is because the Inuit people believe women's bodies are better able to receive the inuas' spiritual energy (Boekholt, 2021). Becoming a shaman in Inuit culture was the ideal route for any woman who wanted more power and independence in her life. It was also very hard to become a shaman, though, regardless of gender. Hence, not very many women were able to pursue this path.

What of these women, then? What role did Inuit beliefs and customs assign to them? For the most part, women were confined to the domestic sphere, yet again, if they were not shamans. The tribal council, which made all the important decisions for the tribe, was made up exclusively of men. The only woman that could influence this council's decision was a shaman and no one else.

Aside from running the ruling council, men were expected to hunt. All Inuit hunters were typically male. Women, meanwhile, remained at home, and they were charged with processing, cooking, and preserving the food that was hunted, on top of doing all the housework. One interesting thing to note here is that, unlike some cultures and beliefs, men were allowed to help with household chores, though they were by no means expected to do so.

However, all this does not mean that Inuit women were oppressed in society. While they generally could not take part in decision-making processes, men and women were thought to be "partners" in society. In others, women's roles were not defined as "subordinate" to that of men. This is why women were given the crucial task of making clothes and armor, a vital skill to have in excessively cold weather and for protecting the hunters of the tribe. Clothes-making was no easy feat. Instead, it was a difficult, arduous, and painstaking process involving multiple steps. It went hand in hand with shelter construction, which was another duty given to women. This meant that women had to have very firm architecture and insulating knowledge.

That women were tasked with such challenging things means that they were neither seen as weak nor as delicate. Instead, they were seen as strong and true partners to their spouses. Perhaps that is why women had the same right as men to ask for a divorce. It was not just the Inuit society that tasked women with more challenging responsibilities and thus gave them a broader role than that of their contemporaries. Other Native American cultures and tribes, like the Apache, did the same.

Core Apache Beliefs

Animistic and shamanistic like other Native tribes, the Apache believed that their ancestor's spirits lived on in the trees, wind, rivers, and other forces of nature. These spirits were the guiding forces of their lives (Meier, n.d.). This belief, once more, resulted in the Apache showing great reverence for nature. They also held great respect for their ancestors. The Apache's primary method of communicating with the spirits was ritualistic dance. Dance was used for all sorts of purposes, including as a healing method and for summoning rain in dry seasons. It was even used to celebrate a woman's first cycle, an important turning point in her life. This celebration was very important in the community because the Apache believed that women became more powerful when they entered puberty. This had a lot to do with the greatly revered and elevated position women held in society, but more on that momentarily.

The Apache maintained that they lived among supernatural powers, which could, at times, be bestowed upon or used by specific individuals. Chief among such people were those that were able to use supernatural healing abilities. More often than not, these people became shamans or medicine men. As religious leaders in their community, they, thus, were charged with conducting important ceremonies and healing rituals.

Role of Apache Women

The Apache actively celebrates when a woman has her first menstrual cycle. This is because they believe that women become a lot stronger upon entering puberty, as you now know. This celebration is called the Sunrise Dance, and it is meant to prepare women for motherhood and family life. In the past, the Sunrise Dance used to last for four days. The Apache believed that the celebrated woman would have an increased power to incite rainfall and heal others for four days following the Sunrise Dance.

So, why is a woman's coming of age, so to speak, so important in the Apache belief system? It is because Apache women are considered to be the "Keepers of the Way" (Burns, 2023). Being a "Keeper of the Way" means being the one to pass down the traditions, beliefs, and culture of your tribe. That Apache women are the Keepers of the Way, then, means that they are charged with passing down the stories, myths, customs, traditions, and beliefs of their tribe, individual families, and bands to the following generation. This is a key part of the role that Apache beliefs ascribed to women.

This is not the only task that was given to women in Apache society, of course. Women are also in charge of nurturing and raising their families. Interestingly enough, daughters are considered more valuable than sons in Apache culture, and mothers must take specific care of raising them as the next "Keepers of the Way." Aside from the expected role of "mother," women are the clothes makers of the tribe. They make all the household items, too, meaning they are the essential craftsmen or, rather, craftswomen of their society. On top of that, they do the food prep, tanning, and preserving.

Within the religious sphere, women are allowed to become shamans and to attend religious ceremonies alongside men. More importantly, they are allowed and even expected to take part in council meetings and are able to influence the decisions of their tribes, bands, and families.

Apache women, then, seemingly had never-ending responsibilities and did a staggering amount for their communities and families. They have broader responsibilities and, thus, a broader role. While gender roles are stringent in Apache culture, women are arguably freer and, like Inuit women, seem to be partners to their male counterparts instead of being subservient to them. All this is very in keeping with the general role that Native American women occupy in different indigenous cultures and belief systems.

While different tribes and cultures have different ways of looking at women, one key commonality among indigenous religions is that they consider women to be integral parts of the societies they live in. The roles that are assigned to them, therefore, tend to be broader and more equal, even if they are typically gendered.

Looking at a broad array of tribes and cultures, it is easy to see that women were able to take on any number of roles and responsibilities. They could become shamans, healers, artists, and even lawmakers and leaders, depending on which tribe you were looking at (*Women's issues*, n.d.). Numerous elder women have sat in village councils among the Haudenosaunee tribes, for instance. Meanwhile, in other tribes, various women, like the famous Wampanoag, were able to become chiefs and lead their tribes in battle. In the Lakota tribe, women were allowed to become warriors and hunters if they wanted.

In essence, then, the role women played in Native American religions and cultures were both broader and heavy with the burden of responsibility. At the same time, this role gave women both greater freedom and more respect compared to some other societies.

Part IV:

New Religious Movements

Chapter 10:

Women in Wicca

"Witchcraft" has long existed in the human lexicon. Various religions have made references to witchcraft, and witches even used to be burned in the past. The Salem Witch Hunts were a prime and terrifying example of this. That being the case, it is a little strange to see a religion whose members call themselves "witches" or "Wiccans." Yet this makes an abundance of sense when you learn even just a little bit of information about Wicca. What could be more natural for a religion that focuses on and honors a female goddess, rather than a male god, to reclaim a word that has historically been used to brutally suppress women and use it as a tool of empowerment instead?

A Quick History of Wicca

Wicca is currently the largest modern pagan religion in the world. The practitioners of Wicca are officially known as Wiccans but fully identify as witches. Wicca initially emerged in the United Kingdom in the 1950s. Since then, it has spread around the globe, and it is surmised that there are a couple of hundred thousand Wiccans around the world these days (Melton, 2018). The real origins of the religion, however, can be traced back to a British civil servant called Gerald Brosseau Gardner. As the story goes, Gerald spent the grand majority of his career in various parts of Asia. He returned to the United Kingdom in the 1930s and came across a band of witches in a forest in England in 1939. These witches taught him a lot about their beliefs and practices, and it is their teachings that formed the basis of the religion that would come to be known as Wicca.

The timing seems to have worked fortuitously for Gardner in that British laws banning witches and witchcraft were revoked in 1951. This gave Gardner the opportunity he needed to write and publish *Witchcraft Today*, which came out in 1954 and introduced the larger public to Wicca for the first time (Brosseau Gardner, 1954). While *Witchcraft Today* was many people's first introduction to Wicca, it is not considered the official, sacred text of the religion. In fact, Wicca does not have a holy text the same way some other religions do.

Following the publication of his book, Gardner established a coven of followers and further developed Wicca into its current format with the help of High Priestess Doreen Valiente. In time, other iterations and versions of Wicca emerged. In the 60s and 70s, it rapidly spread across the United States as part of the emerging counterculture. From there, even more iterations of Wicca grew.

The Core Beliefs of Wicca

At its core, Wicca is a nature-based religion in that Wiccan worship Mother Nature and Father Sky. Different Wiccans choose different deities from across the world to worship (*Wicca*, 2019). Wiccans meet in groups called covens. Contrary to typical, Christian-based understandings of witchcraft, Wiccans are not Satanic worshipers in any way. They do not worship the devil. They do, however, use magic and witchcraft, which is why they call themselves "witches."

When Wiccans refer to magic, they are referring to the universal energy around them. The belief here is that they can use this universal energy to affect the world around them and, thus, obtain the end results that they would like. When using magic, most Wiccans use something called the Threefold Rule. This rule dictates that

- Positive magic cast on someone other than the self will come back to the caster and deliver three times the benefit to the caster.

- Negative magic cast on someone other than the self will come back to the caster and deliver three times the damage to the caster.

This is an important rule in Wicca as it emphasizes actions and consequences while stressing a sense of personal responsibility. In other words, it is kind of the epitome of "you reap what you sow."

To channel universal energy to cast magic, Wiccans use all manner of techniques such as dance, hypnosis, chants, and visualization. The idea here is to focus their psychic energy through these actions and direct it toward their purpose, which may be to heal someone, help someone, or even protect someone. While Wicca can be used to heal others, the majority of the community stresses that healing magic should be done alongside traditional medical practices, not instead of them.

On top of all this, Wiccans believe in reincarnation. They tend to be vegetarians, given the respect they show to Mother Earth, though they do not have to be. They do not have a central leadership system in the form of clergymen and the like, though covens do elect First Officers, who typically serve their covens for one to two terms. Some covens also have High Priestesses and High Priests, who are tasked with teaching initiates about their new faith. On the whole, Wicca is a fairly democratic belief system and an entirely free and accepting one at that.

Women in Wicca

Of all the religions out there, Wicca may just be the most equal and feminist one. This fact is all too clear and visible considering Wicca's reclaiming of the word "witch." Historically, "witch" was used as a tool of persecution for women at worst and as an insult at best. By taking back the word "witch," Wiccan women essentially identify with the nine million victims of past witch hunts and reclaim their right to be powerful (Doyle, 2015).

Wicca's feminist bent is not just obvious in its language choice, though. The fact that it is a religion heavy on goddess worship is another major bit of proof of this. There are multiple goddesses that Wiccans can worship in Wicca, and most of its iterations tend to be more matriarchal. One stark difference between Wicca and other religions is the lack of sin and shame (Floyd, 2017). In most religions, women are expected to be pure and virginal before they get married and loyal and faithful after they get married, as you have seen. This, however, is not the case in Wicca. Women are free to live out their sexuality however they choose, regardless of whether they are married or not.

The general idea of Wicca is built on "if it does not hurt anyone, then go ahead and do it." This applies to living out your life and sexuality however you choose. This is why, for example, homosexuality is not condemned in Wicca either, the way it is in some other religions. Wiccan women are free to enter into same-sex relationships and marriages, as are Wiccan men. Wicca is even known to be widely accepting of genders outside the traditional gender binary, meaning "men" and "women." With all that being the case, that Wicca is devoid of the concept of shame and sin is not surprising at all.

There is a common misconception that Wicca is a fertility religion. This, however, is not true, especially not considering how many different versions of Wicca there are. Sadly, this often causes a limited understanding of Wiccan women. Some people, thus, conclude that Wiccan women's roles are largely confined to that of mothers. The truth cannot be more different. Wiccan women are free to pursue whatever path they choose in life, be it motherhood, successful, childless careers, or something else. This is because Wicca recognizes women as the independent, strong individuals that they are. It stresses their nurturing and intuitive characteristics, as well as emotional intelligence, but presents these as strengths, not traits that make them fit for the domestic sphere alone.

Wiccan Women, the "Goddess" and Rituals

A lot of Wiccans consider the "goddess" as a sort of champion for women's rights (Shuler, 2012). As such, the goddess is a symbol of strength, freedom, and empowerment. That Wicca values the figure of the goddess, though, does not mean that it disregards the masculine or considers it to be unimportant. In fact, Wicca specifically states that the goddess and god, the feminine and the masculine, are of equal value. Neither is more dominant than the other, and neither is subservient to the other. That the goddess is valued over god in Wicca is another common misconception about Wicca, which causes some to turn away from it without developing a proper understanding of the religion.

More often than not, these rituals worship two specific deities: the triple goddess and the three-horned god. The triple goddess is known as the Maiden, Mother, and Crone. The Maiden represents youth and innocence. The Mother represents power, stability, fertility, and nurturing, and the Crone represents wisdom and, ultimately, death. In other words, the Triple Goddess stands for the three stages of life that every woman will follow (*Wicca beliefs and practices*, n.d.).

Meanwhile, the Triple-Horned God is the male counterpart to the Triple Goddess and stands for adventure, male virility, and strength. Both the Triple Goddess and the Triple-Horned God are worshiped equally in Wicca, be it in Wiccans' day-to-day lives and practices or during rituals. The greatest bit of evidence of the fact that Wicca places equal value on the goddess and the god can be seen in its rituals. Wiccan rituals traditionally take place around an altar, with the participants forming a circle around it. This very positioning stresses equality as no one gets a superior view to others.

A typical ritual begins with the forming of a circle around the altar, which has two candles on it (Shuler, 2012). The candles represent the fire element and are accompanied by items that represent other elements, like incense for air, grains of the earth, and a bowl of water. There might be other items on the altar as well, specific to the ritual that will be conducted. The enacted rituals may take different shapes and forms—for instance, it can be done with a large group or solo— but it always pays equal attention and importance to the Maiden, Mother, Crone, and the Triple Horned God. During rituals, the High Priestess plays the part of the goddess, while the High Priest plays the part of the god. In this sense, the rituals are somewhat theatrical, and the attention given to the deities is immediately visible.

What all this means is this: While Wicca is a very empowering and freeing religion for women, it is not one that is in any way diminishing for men. It does not expand women's role to the detriment of the man's. Instead, it seeks to balance them out. In doing so, it frees men and women of constrictions that may have been imposed on them by the societies they live in and the gender expectations that are placed on them.

Chapter 11:

Women in the New Age Movement

A lot of people think that Wicca is part of the New Age Movement, which has been gaining more and more traction in recent years. This, however, is not entirely true. While there are a number of similarities between Wicca and the New Age Movement, the two are not the same for the very simple reason that they came into being at different points in time. Wicca's roots go back to the 1930s, though it was officially created in the 1950s. The New Age Movement, on the other hand, did not blossom and started sweeping across the globe until well into the 1970s and 1980s (Melton, 2019).

It is entirely possible for this to be your first time hearing about the New Age Movement, considering how "young" it is. What exactly is the New Age Movement, then? Truthfully, the movement can be defined as the gathering and rise of a number of metaphysical and occult communities. It is a movement that is made up of an eclectic set of beliefs and religious practices that seem to combine spirituality with therapeutic approaches. They also seem to harbor elements of Taoism, Buddhism, clairvoyance, tarot, paganism, and psychology. These beliefs and practices were officially labeled the New Age Movement in the 1990s by sociologists and social psychologists such as Paul Heelas.

Discussing the New Age Movement can, at times, be difficult because the wide array of beliefs that are part of the movement neither have specific, unchangeable names, like Islam or Taoism, nor official doctrines and sacred books. Instead, they are collages of different beliefs and interpretations, changing from individual to individual. This does not mean, however, that they are impossible to discuss. It also does not mean understanding women's role and place in the New Age Movement is all that hard to do. To accomplish this, you simply need to understand the unifying elements, that is to say, the commonalities, between the spiritual beliefs making up the New Age Movement. You can then easily trace women's role and place in it.

A Quick History of the New Age Movement

The thing about the New Age Movement is that it is not a single creed, belief system, or institution. Rather it is a movement that harbors a collage of different beliefs, all of which have certain similar ideas but differ on many other points. The adherents of the New Age Movement are known as New Agers. New Agers typically hold beliefs that focus on spiritual enlightenment, harmony, and spiritual transformation of some sort (Dunn, n.d.). The reason the movement that these people belong to is known as the New Age is that these beliefs are a part of the coming era of light, love, healing, and transformation on both the individual and societal levels. New Agers believe that through this movement, a world that is rife with poverty, war, racism, and many other dire problems can be transformed into one where peace, love, acceptance, abundance, and other positive sentiments reign supreme.

While the New Age began spreading across the United States and then the world in the 1970s and 1980s, its origins go much farther than that.

This is because a lot of the concepts and ideas that the beliefs making up the New Age are built on concepts and ideas from Hinduism, Gnosticism, occultism, and more. Gnosticism is a religion that holds the belief that human beings harbor a divine spark, that is to say, a piece of God himself, within them (Denova, 2021). Occultism, on the other hand, is a conglomeration of supernatural beliefs that fall outside the domain of traditional religions (Gilbert, 2019). In any case, because the roots of the beliefs making up the New Age Movement can be traced all the way back to the 2nd century C.E. in some, the movement itself can be considered older than it officially is (Dunn, n.d.).

The New Age Movement does not have a sacred book or text to speak of or any kind of real, hierarchical structure since it began spreading across the world in the modern era. As such, it should not be surprising to hear that the New Age Movement primarily used the power of technology and media to reach new believers to add to its ranks. From books to television programs, websites to Instagram channels, there are now just too many New Age Movement mediums out there to count. That being the case, it is estimated that currently, there are between 20,000 to 6 million adherents of the New Age Movement in the United States alone (Heelas, 2005, p. 112).

The Core Beliefs of the New Age Movement

There are a lot of different beliefs to be found in the New Age Movement, as was said before. Among these, the most influential have been Gnosticism, occultism, New Thought, Spiritualism, Theosophy, and the Human Potential Movement. Gnosticism is the belief that everyone harbors a piece of God within themselves, as mentioned previously (Denova, 2021). These divine sparks are independent of the human bodies they are trapped in, which are condemned to eventual decay. They need to acquire true knowledge, which is referred to as gnosis, given to them by a source that falls out of the purview of the material world if they want to discover their true potential and status.

Occultism is a gathering of practices and theories that involve the use of various supernatural forces, as you have seen (Gilbert, 2019). These practices enable the practitioners to alter and manipulate the laws of nature, using such things as magic. Then there is New Thought. The

New Thought Religious Movement is a healing movement that is based on certain metaphysical beliefs and assumptions (*New Thought religious movement*, n.d.). While the beliefs that New Thought puts forward are very varied, the general idea is that the "truth" is something that is being revealed to humankind constantly and that there can never be a final human authority on what "truth" ultimately is.

Another defining belief in the New Age Movement is Spiritualism. Spiritualism is the religious belief that the souls of the deceased are capable of interacting with the living in a number of different ways (Melton, 2013). Typically, this communication is done with the help of an experienced medium who possesses the ability to reach out to and commune with these spirits. The very idea of Spiritualism is naturally centered around the concept of an immortal spirit that survives and transcends the death and decay of the physical form.

Of course, there is also Theosophy, which can be considered a kind of occult movement too. Theosophy states that there is a deeper spiritual reality to be accessed in the world (Melton, 2020). You can access this spiritual reality by using a couple of different methods, such as meditation, revelation, and transcendence, depending on what form of Theosophy you are an adherent of.

Finally, there is the Human Potential Movement, which can be defined as a psychological and psychotherapeutic approach that promotes spontaneous living, sensitivity, personal growth, and spiritual independence. Essentially, it is a seven-step path an individual is supposed to take to fulfill their true and full potential (Kiesling, 2020).

There are a great many more beliefs that are part of the compendium of the New Age Movement. While all of these beliefs are, clearly, very different, they do have some commonalities. The key things they have in common are that (Dunn, n.d.)

- they reject the belief of traditional, monotheistic religions and their assertion that there is only one God.

- they are united in their belief that everything is one and that God can be found in everything and everyone.

- there is a divine aspect, meaning a piece of god, in every individual.

- every human being is personally responsible for developing this divine aspect within.

- by developing their divine aspect, a person can effectively help transform the reality and world around them, thereby helping to create harmony in the world.

Women's Role in the New Age Movement

A lot of observers, particularly academicians, have noticed that the New Age Movement has been attracting a lot of women in recent years. The different beliefs making up the movement seem to be incredibly appealing to women from all walks of life. This has understandably provoked the question, "Why?" What is it about the New Age Movement that makes it such a go-to for women? The reason for this is quite simple: Women are attracted to the New Age because the role the movement ascribes to them is far more independent and freer of gender roles than any other religion out there, with the possible exception of Wicca.

The freedom that characterizes women's role in the New Age Movement is easy enough to see. Take the question of "women's sexuality," for example. Most religions expect women to be pure, chaste, and, if possible, virginal, as we have seen. There are very few religions and belief systems that allow women to explore their own sexuality and the ones that do only permit them to do so after they have been securely married. Contrary to these religions, the New Age Movement does not place such expectations on women. At the same time, it puts specific emphasis on acceptance and openness where gender, as well as sexuality, are concerned (*Gender and sexuality*, n.d.). Put simply, then, the New Age Movement gives people the freedom and ability to explore their sexuality and gender outside the traditional binary without feeling like they are disconnecting from or losing their faith. That right there is one of the most appealing facets of the New Age Movement for many women.

The main reason the New Age Movement is so accepting of women's exploration of their own sexuality is that it views sex as a positive thing, even when it is done for reasons other than procreation. This is decidedly unlike a lot of religions that equate sex for pleasure with sin and shame, especially if it is done out of wedlock. Again, contrary to such religions, the New Age Movement sees sex as a form of self-expression. This is applicable to all types of sex between all types of people. In the movement, then, sex is a vehicle for spiritual awakening, awareness, and even enlightenment.

One reason that the New Age Movement is so open and accepting with regard to sexuality and gender is that it started gaining momentum during the second wave of feminism of the 60s and 70s. The second-wave feminists of the time were all about challenging the gender hierarchies that existed in their societies, along with gender norms. Equally as importantly, they pushed for a woman's right to control her own body and sexuality. In other words, sexual freedom was a hot topic among second-wave feminists, and this emphasis became a part of the New Age Movement.

This is not the only way in which the second-wave feminists influenced the New Age Movement, though. When you think about it, the second-wave feminists had a huge impact on all religions. Women of different faiths were looking for gender equality within their own belief systems at the time. This meant pushing for things like their religious institutions allowing women to be ordained, altering male-focused language of their belief systems so that it became more gender-neutral, and creating women-centric spaces for ritual and worship. These religious rights that these women were fighting for were picked up by the New Age Movement and very quickly became a part of it. This made the movement a far more welcoming and accepting system and environment for women and started to draw them toward itself.

Another reason why the New Age Movement is so popular among women has to do with its understanding of gender roles. As a modern belief system, the New Age Movement is one of the few religions that does not confine women's role in society to the domestic sphere. Instead, it recognizes that modern women can become anything they want to become, be it a pilot, artist, housewife, stand-up comedian, biochemical engineer, or something else entirely. This accomplishes two things. First, it respects women's freedom to choose their own path without feeling like they have to conform to any expectations. Second, it prevents them from experiencing a sort of double alienation within their own families as a result of the dissatisfaction they may feel in their prescribed role as mother, wife, and caregiver (Thompson, 2018). In other words, the New Age Movement allows women to explore their own identities more freely while holding tight to their self-worth.

One of the things that the New Age Movement typically advises women to do is to discover their "authentic selves." This can mean any number of things for any number of people. For some, their authentic self really might be happy as a housewife and mother of three. For others, their authentic self might be a solo backpacker, working mom, or single mother who is also the CEO of a Fortune 500 company. The appeal of the New Age Movement is that, because it does not have a strict definition of what a woman's role should be, it gives women the room they need to explore what their authentic selves are like.

Chapter 12:

A Summary of Findings

Looking at the religions of the world one after the other, two things become immediately clear. The first is that world religions have had some very specific things to say about women and their role in their faith, families, societies, and the world. Curiously, there are a lot of commonalities in what all these religions have to say about women and their roles. The second thing is that as times and expectations change, it seems women's prescribed roles have started to change as well. This change was brought on both by the changing needs of the world and through the painstaking efforts of faithful women intent on living and practicing their faith on their own terms. As a result of these women's efforts, not only have certain changes taken place in centuries-old religions, but new religions and belief systems have arisen as well. These belief systems naturally have their roots in older religions but have adopted less rigid definitions of women's roles, as well as a variety of other matters. These developments in different faiths and the rise of new belief systems prove two things: that religion is not an inherently inalterable concept and that women can expand the space that is given to them without denying their faith.

The Commonalities Between Religions

There are a surprising number of commonalities among the religions of the world, at least where women's role in them is concerned. Take the Abrahamic religions, for instance, meaning Judaism, Christianity, and Islam, respectively. Traditionally, these religions have ascribed the role of wife, mother, and caregiver to women. As a result, their role was confined to the domestic sphere, meaning either their father's or their husband's house. This role and the arena in which it was lived came with certain expectations and judgments with regard to women's characters. For instance, women were expected to be obedient and subservient to their husbands, as well as to other men, at all times. This point was driven home in stories such as that of Miriam, who was punished for speaking out against Moses.

At the same time, women were expected to be devout and loyal to their husbands. Sarah was the prime example of spousal loyalty since she was loyal enough to ask her husband to sleep with someone else so that they could have a child. She was also loyal enough to refuse a Pharaoh, with some angelic help, of course, since she was already married. It seems both Judaism and Christianity expected women to be wives, mothers, loyal, obedient, and subservient to men. Christianity also expected women to be pure as the driven snow. This was doubly important given their status as "temptresses," which was emphasized in the story of Eve. She was considered to be responsible for the original sin, after all. This was the reason why women were punished with always being subservient to men. It is also why women were discouraged from speaking their minds in some sects and areas of Christianity.

Interestingly enough, the story of the original sin was told a little differently in Islam in that Islam did not make Eve the sole guilty party in the story. Rather it stressed that Adam and Eve were equally at fault for what happened. While this did not absolve Eve of guilt, it prevented the story from giving the message that Eve was solely to blame for humankind's expulsion from Eden. This is not the only point at which Islam seems to differ from Christianity and Judaism. For example, the Qur'an is home to numerous suras that declare women to be the equals of men. Yet for all that, Islam, too, seems to have ascribed a largely domestic role to women. While it has given women more rights than other religions of its time, it has still expected women to be obedient and subservient to their men. It has still defined their primary role as that of mother and wife.

This seems to be an ongoing trend since that same role is featured prominently in Hinduism. As part of this role, they are expected to remain chaste, loyal, and pure. They are expected to be devoted wives to their husbands. This is nowhere better exemplified than in Lakshmi's decision to reincarnate into the world as Sita so that she can be with her husband again. In exchange for this kind of loyalty, however, women are promised a great degree of respect and reverence. Aside from that, once they are married, women are allowed to explore their sexuality and even encouraged to do so if the story of the Kama Sutra is anything to go by.

This same sexual freedom is not afforded to women in Buddhism, though. Buddhism can be slightly controversial to women in that there are schools of thought in it that both define women's roles in very constraining ways and look at them with a rather problematic lens. Such schools of thought believe women will need to reincarnate as men in their next lives to achieve dharma. While not all schools of thought in Buddhism hold this view, traditional Buddhism itself does have two ways of seeing women: as maternal sources of anguish and as lustful temptresses. This view is likely to blame for that rather unfortunate reincarnation idea.

The good news, as you'll remember, is that not all Buddhist schools see women in such limited ways. The Buddha himself, for example, recognized that women were just as capable of seeing the Truth as men were. This is why he eventually allowed women to enter into the order and become Buddhist nuns. When you think about it, this means women were allowed into the Order in Buddhism before Christian women were allowed to become clergy. Of course, women were still expected to remain subservient to men, even in Buddhism. Buddhist nuns were even expected to take seven additional vows when entering into the Order to ensure that. That, at least, seems to be one thing that Buddhism has in common with Abrahamic religions, as well as religions like Hinduism.

Buddhism has this in common with Taoism as well, which is a very interesting Eastern religion in and of itself. The feminine, that is to say, the yin, is a huge part of Taoism, after all. Taoism is about the balance between the yin and the yang, the feminine and the masculine, as you'll remember. This balance, however, still necessitates that the woman takes on a domestic role as a wife, mother, and caregiver. More and more, this role appears to be emblematic of patriarchal religions, so it is not all that surprising that Taoism is not an exception. Unlike other religions, like Buddhism, for instance, Taoism believes women are more easily able to connect with the Tao. This is why they are easily given the responsibility of educating others about the Tao and why they are allowed to become priests, just as Buddhist women are allowed to become nuns.

One thing that Taoism has in common with Hinduism, another Eastern religion, is that it allows women to explore their sexuality, once they are married, to a startling degree. As you'll recall, the Taoists were the first sexologists in history. As important as this fact is, though, it does not change the fact that women were mostly expected to stay in their homes. Neither does it change the fact that not a lot of women were able to become priests, given the lack of educational opportunities provided to them. Of course, women pioneers like Sun Bu-Er changed that for a lot of women, but that does not mean Taoism was able to achieve true equality in the practical realm between men and women, where their gender roles were concerned.

Taoism is somewhat similar to Confucianism, which makes an abundance of sense, seeing as both religions or religious philosophies, if you will, emerged in Ancient China around the same time. Like Taoism, Confucianism believed in yin and yang. Unlike Taoism, however, Confucianism did not have very much to say about women's sexuality other than women should only be with their husbands and be pure and chaste. Loyalty in a wife, the expected role of a woman in Confucian ideology, was a given, as was motherhood.

One thing Confucianism absolutely demanded of women was filial piety, which is understandable, seeing as family was at the very center of Confucianist thought. Filial piety for women meant they were to devote themselves to their families. Most women were thus not allowed to pursue much of an education; however, Confucianism created an interesting educational opportunity for women. Numerous Confucianist works were written for women and sometimes even by women and for women. This promoted female readership and writership in an era when literacy was expressly the domain of men, no less. Perhaps this is why, despite having strict gender roles, Confucianism never once implied that women were inferior—intellectually, morally, or otherwise—to men the way some religions, such as certain schools of Buddhist thought, did.

If you are looking for religions where women adopt more expansive and flexible roles, it is the traditional African and Native American religions you have to look to. While there are far too many tribes in the continent of Africa and, therefore, far too many different belief systems to look at, it is easy to see that these systems have similar points of view where women are concerned. Like with the other religions we have seen, traditional African religions ascribe the role of mother and wife to women. However, the responsibilities given to women as part of these roles can often be more expansive than those that they are given in other religions. For instance, in many African cultures and belief systems, women are allowed to become shamans and medicine women. The same goes for the privileges that are afforded to women. For instance, in Igbo and Yoruba cultures, women are actually allowed to enter into same-sex marriages, something many other religions would actively ban and even condemn. At the same time, women are able to participate in governing decisions, depending on which traditional African culture and belief system you are dealing with. The Umu Inyon of the Igbo people is a prime example of this.

Traditional African religions are not the only belief systems that allow women to take a larger part in the society they live in. Native American cultures and religions do so as well. In Native American religions, women are allowed to be more than mothers and wives and can even become chiefs in some tribes and bands, as you may remember. Like in traditional African religions, the responsibilities that come with women's roles are far more expansive than those of some other religions. Among the Inuits, for example, it is the women that have to preserve the food, build shelters the way architects would, and make both clothing and armor as genuine craftswomen. The same goes for Apache women, who, in a striking difference from most world religions, are the heads of their families rather than the men they were married to. They are also the Keepers of the Way, meaning that it is Apache women that are in charge of passing on their beliefs, culture, and customs to the following generations, an immense responsibility, whichever way you look at it.

Clearly, then, "delicate" and "weak" were not characteristics ascribed to Native American women in the belief systems and cultures that they were a part of. This is one major thing they have in common with some of the newer religious movements, such as Wicca and the New Age Movement. Out of all the religions we have seen thus far, Wicca is the one that bears the least amount of similarity to the others. This is evident in the fact that its practitioners claim to be witches since witchcraft and witches are things that religions like Christianity actively condemn. This is not the only difference to be found between Wicca and other world religions, though. There's also the fact that Wicca does not state that women's primary role is that of mother and wife. Instead, Wicca is about female empowerment and equality between men and women. This is evident in all that Wicca does, including its rituals and the way they are acted out.

In this regard, Wicca is certainly similar to the New Age Movement. It can even be considered a part of the New Age Movement, depending on how you look at things. The collage of beliefs making up the New Age Movement is all about making it possible for people—not just women, but everyone—to find their authentic selves. As such, this belief system does not ascribe any concrete, defined, or rigid role to women. Instead, it urges them to explore their own spirituality on their own terms. It advocates for sexual freedom, and in this, it is similar to Hinduism and Taoism, with one vital difference. Religions like Hinduism and Taoism allow for sexual exploration post-marriage, whereas the New Age Movement embraces sex as a wholly positive thing, both pre- and post-marriage. As such, it encourages women to explore and discover their sexuality at whatever point in time and in whichever form they'd like.

This, obviously, is something that sets the New Age Movement apart from many religions, as is its emphasis on women's freedom. For all that, the New Age Movement is different from other world religions, though, it is also quite similar to them. After all, the roots of the significant number of the beliefs that make up the New Age Movement can be traced back to other world religions such as Gnosticism and occultism. You can even trace these roots back to Hinduism, Taoism, Buddhism, and Abrahamic religions, among others.

Conclusion

So, what does all this mean for women's role in world religions going forward? First, while it is true that many of the world's religions have determined women's role as that of mother and wife, this role seems to be evolving. Evidence of this fact is clear to see in all religions you look at. Jewish women have actively been pursuing careers in an array of different fields, including politics. They have also been pursuing their education, both religious and academic. Both of these were things that Jewish women had traditionally been barred from doing. A similar thing has been happening in Christianity, with devout, even conservative women becoming judges, lawyers, and politicians, citing Deborah's prolific career from the Bible to any that dare question their decision. In Islam, women have waged battles to achieve the true equality that is promised to them in their own faith.

Meanwhile, Hindu women have been breaking out of their "support role" molds and taking on jobs, earning their own money, and holding their own properties for a number of years now. Buddhist women have been working hard in the past centuries and even today to change some of the more problematic attitudes some schools of Buddhism harbor toward women. Furthermore, they have been working hard to join the Order as nuns and have even been instrumental in the creation of variations of Buddhism, like Tibetan Buddhism and Tantric Buddhism, that make greater room for women in the faith they are a part of.

The same can be said of Taoism, seeing as the resurgence of the religion is actually owed to the women who embraced it again and began spreading it like the teachers that Taoism saw them as. Even Confucianism, which has some very strict gender roles, seems to have opened up a little in modern times. After all, it was women scholars who unearthed Confucianism's contribution to women's education and used it as a starting point for a conversation about women's education in more conservative societies.

As for the indigenous religions, the changes that these belief systems have undergone have been a little more different. This is because these religions and the cultures that they are a part of have had to resist Western influences to some degree and preserve their customs throughout the centuries. It is undeniable, though, that women have played a crucial part in this. They have not only played a major role in preserving their own traditions, but they have managed to keep passing them along to future generations in a way that accommodates the changing gender roles of the time.

Lastly, there are the New Religious Movements, such as Wicca and the New Age Movement. One undeniable truth about these religions is that, unlike the grand majority of the religions we have covered in this book, they are not patriarchal belief systems. They, therefore, do not perpetrate ideas born out of a patriarchal world. Instead, they have become religions that honor women's equality with men and seek to give them the freedom they need to discover their authentic selves.

What is the overall fate of world religions then, and the fate of women's ultimate role? One school of thought here is that the New Religious Movement will continue to draw more and more adherents, especially female believers to it in this increasingly secular world. As a result, fewer and fewer women will identify with the more traditional religions we are familiar with. While these religions will not wither away, they will shrink. Another school of thought is that the religions of the world, much like the New Religious Movement, will keep on evolving. As part of this process, women's roles and how women are generally perceived will evolve and change as well.

Thus, these religions will retain their core beliefs, but the role they ascribe to women will allow them to discover and express their authentic selves as well. Considering how much different religions and women's roles in them have already changed, I am more inclined to believe that the latter, rather than the former, will ultimately happen. While it is true that nothing that remains static in the world can persist for long, upon reading *Women's Role in World Religions*, it is clear that religions are not exactly static. Rather they are being pushed toward change by pioneering and devout women who are willing to preserve and protect their faith even as they redefine their roles in it.

Historically speaking, the role that world religions have offered to women has been rather narrow. As such, many women struggled with the parts they were expected to play, finding it difficult to make themselves fit into the molds they had been given. So, they took matters into their own hands and started pushing the boundaries and limits around them. At times, their efforts did not seem to pay off, and they were apparently punished like Miriam was. As the years went by, however, more and more women seemed to join their ranks.

Some of these women, like Sun Bu-Er and Mary Magdalene, we have met throughout the course of this book, but they were by no means alone. Take a look around the world today, and you can find many of their companions. There's Reverend Dr. Katharine Jefferts Schori, who is the 26th Bishop of the Episcopal Church. A century or two ago, a woman becoming the bishop of a church, let alone the Episcopal Church, would have been akin to unthinkable. There's Jetsunma Tenzin Palmo, the Buddhist nun who founded the Dongyu Gatsal Ling Nunnery, which is based in India. Considering some Buddhist attitudes toward women, it can objectively be said that managing to open a new nunnery is a feat all its own. It is only by adding more and more women to the monastic ranks that such attitudes will ever successfully change.

In all honesty, the list can go on and on. The point, of course, is that it is thanks to the valiant efforts of the women of the past that such women are able to continue working within their respective faiths to keep pushing the boundaries around them. What's more, it is thanks to such women that both the religions of the world and the place of women in the world will keep evolving.

Thank you for reading *Women's Role in World Religions*. I hope that you have found this book to be informative and enlightening and see it as food for thought. If you have, please leave a review and share your thoughts!

References

Africa traditional religious system as basis of understanding Christian spiritual warfare. (2000, August 22). Lausanne Movement. https://lausanne.org/content/west-african-case-study

Ahuvia, M. (n.d.). *Who are Jews? An overview of Jewish history from ancient times on, and the origins of antisemitism.* UW Stroum Center for Jewish Studies. https://jewishstudies.washington.edu/who-are-jews-jewish-history-origins-antisemitism/

Al Khayat, M. H. (2003). *Woman in Islam and her role in human development.* https://applications.emro.who.int/dsaf/dsa312.pdf

Aliyu, R. (2018, May 15). *Woman-woman marriage in Pre-Colonial Igboland.* The Rustin Times. https://therustintimes.com/2018/05/15/woman-woman-marriage-in-pre-colonial-igboland-revised/#:~:text=The%20ancestral%20marriage%20is%20not

Ānandajoti, B. (2015, March). 05. *The story about the elder nun Dhammadinna.* Ancient Buddhist Texts. https://www.ancient-buddhist-texts.net/English-Texts/Foremost-Elder-Nuns/05-Dhammadinna.htm

Appleton, S., & Willis, M. (2022, May 20). *Confucianism.* National Geographic Society. https://education.nationalgeographic.org/resource/confucianism/

Baskin, J. (n.d.). *Women in Rabbinic literature.* My Jewish Learning. https://www.myjewishlearning.com/article/women-in-rabbinic-literature/

Bhattacharyya, K. (2022, February 8). *The relevance of Ma Saraswati in modern education*. The Times of India. https://timesofindia.indiatimes.com/readersblog/herbinger/the-relevance-of-ma-saraswati-in-modern-education-41142/

Boekholt, N. (2021, April 29). *Inuit women: An incredible life of strife and tradition*. Yoair Blog. https://www.yoair.com/blog/inuit-women-an-incredible-life-of-strife-and-tradition/

Bourne, H. (2013, April 2). *Mara, the tempter*. Pacific Mindfulness. https://pacificmindfulness.com/blog/mara-tempter

Brosseau Gardner, G. (1954). *Witchcraft today / Introd. by Margaret Murray*. Citadel Press.

Buddhism: Basic beliefs. (2019). United Religions Initiative. https://www.uri.org/kids/world-religions/buddhist-beliefs

Burns, P. D. (2023, March 1). *Apache women: Keepers of the Way*. Owlcation. https://owlcation.com/social-sciences/Apache-Women-Keepers-of-The-Way

Canby, S. (2021). *The five pillars of Islam*. The Met. https://www.metmuseum.org/learn/educators/curriculum-resources/art-of-the-islamic-world/unit-one/the-five-pillars-of-islam#:~:text=The%20belief%20that%20%22There%20is

Carroll, J. (2006, June). *Who was Mary Magdalene?* Smithsonian Magazine; Smithsonian.com. https://www.smithsonianmag.com/history/who-was-mary-magdalene-119565482/

Chizhik-Goldschmidt, A. (2015, December 25). *Despite decrees, Jewish ultra-Orthodox women still quietly studying for degrees*. Haaretz. https://www.haaretz.com/jewish/2015-12-25/ty-article/.premium/despite-decrees-haredi-women-still-studying-for-degrees/0000017f-f7ba-d887-a7ff-fffe683e0000

Christianity. (2017, October 13). History. A&E Television Networks. https://www.history.com/topics/religion/history-of-christianity

Craven, B. (2018, December). *Following Mary's Example*. Church of Jesus Christ. https://site.churchofjesuschrist.org/study/new-era/2018/12/following-marys-example?lang=eng&adobe_mc_ref=https://www.churchofjesuschrist.org/study/new-era/2018/12/following-marys-example?lang=eng&adobe_mc_sdid=SDID=25252308B043A8A6-4CC34041502F409A

Deities of the Yoruba and Fon religions. (n.d.). Encyclopedia.com. https://www.encyclopedia.com/history/news-wires-white-papers-and-books/deities-yoruba-and-fon-religions

Denova, R. (2021, April 9). *Gnosticism*. World History Encyclopedia. https://www.worldhistory.org/Gnosticism/?gclid=CjwKCAjwjMiiBhA4EiwAZe6jQyCD2ji9XWH8LeiE8OMByMbgcf2YSRCX-Oc0t4XfRclR0wOv-W7PeBoC8iUQAvD_BwE

Dopamu, A. (1999). *Editorial: The Yoruba Religious System*. African Update Archives. https://web.ccsu.edu/afstudy/supdt99.htm

Doyle, S. (2015, February 24). *Season of the witch: why young women are flocking to the ancient craft*. The Guardian; The Guardian. https://www.theguardian.com/world/2015/feb/24/witch-symbol-feminist-power-azealia-banks

Dunn, L. (n.d.). *What is the New Age Movement?* Explore God. https://www.exploregod.com/articles/what-is-the-new-age-movement

The Editors of Encyclopedia Britannica. (2019). *Igbo people*. In Encyclopædia Britannica. Encyclopedia Brittanica

Egbo, N. (2021, June 13). *The life of an Igbo woman pre-colonial times*. The Guardian Nigeria News - Nigeria and World News. https://guardian.ng/life/the-life-of-an-igbo-woman-pre-colonial-times/

Familusi, O. (2012). *African culture and the status of women: The Yorubaexample*. https://www.jpanafrican.org/docs/vol5no1/5.1AfricanCulture .pdf

Federally recognized Indian tribes and resources for Native Americans. (n.d.). USAGov. https://www.usa.gov/tribes#:~:text=The%20federal%20gover nment%20recognizes%20574

Female Hindu deities – the Tridevi - nature of ultimate reality in hinduism. (n.d.). BBC Bitesize. https://www.bbc.co.uk/bitesize/guides/zrf6pbk/revision/5#: ~:text=Tridevi%2C%20or%20three%20goddesses%2C%20is

Fishkoff, S. (2011, May 3). *Jewish women: A chronicle of changes*. Jewish Telegraphic Agency. https://www.jta.org/2011/05/03/lifestyle/jewish-women

Floyd, C. (2017). *Mother goddesses and subversive witches: Competing narratives of gender essentialism, heteronormativity, feminism, and queerness in Wiccan theology and ritual*. Honors Projects. https://digitalcommons.iwu.edu/socanth_honproj/56/

Gayley, H. (2007, December 1). *Who was Yeshe Tsogyal?* Lion's Roar. https://www.lionsroar.com/the-many-lives-of-yeshe-tsogyal/

Gender and sexuality. (n.d.). Patheos. https://www.patheos.com/library/new-age/ethics-morality-community/gender-and-sexuality

Gilbert, R. A. (2019). *Occultism*. In Encyclopædia Britannica. https://www.britannica.com/topic/occultism

Gordon, A. (2003, April). *Yoruba, the*. Harvard Divinity School. https://rpl.hds.harvard.edu/faq/yoruba

Hamel, K. D. (2019, May 23). *The problem of Eve and her Impact on women's roles in ministry*. Katrina D Hamel. https://www.katrinadhamel.com/post/the-problem-of-eve-and-the-modern-woman

Heelas, P. (2005). *The New Age movement: the celebration of the self and the sacralization of modernity*. Blackwell.

Heyrman, C. L. (n.d.). *Native American religion in early America*. University of Delaware National Humanities Center. http://nationalhumanitiescenter.org/tserve/eighteen/ekeyinfo /natrel.htm#:~:text=Second%2C%20most%20native%20peop les%20worshiped

Hinduism 101: Women and Hinduism. (2017, December 6). Hindu American Foundation. https://www.hinduamerican.org/blog/hinduism-101-women-and-hinduism?gclid=CjwKCAjwl6OiBhA2EiwAuUwWZTT-ytTgEPql09dCvteiV4UjAxHQFOFmdBfHEPCpVUCkIHwFE UYqDxoChzYQAvD_BwE&utm_source=google&utm_mediu m=cpc

Holy Bible: Containing the Old and New Testaments: King James Version. (n.d.). American Bible Society.

Hughes, A. (2018, February 14). *"Ramayana": The Indian love story of Rama and Sita*. Yogapedia. https://www.yogapedia.com/ramayana-the-indian-love-story-of-rama-and-sita/2/10217

The Inuit people. (n.d.). Polar Pod. https://www.polarpod.fr/en/encyclopaedia/arctic/6-history-and-geography/5-the-inuit-people

Inuit religious traditions. (n.d.). Encyclopedia.com. https://www.encyclopedia.com/environment/encyclopedias-almanacs-transcripts-and-maps/inuit-religious-traditions

Irwan , U. N. (2018, April 2). *What is the role of a woman in Islam?* Muslim.sg. https://www.muslim.sg/articles/what-is-the-role-of-a-woman-in-islam

Jones, E., & Chamberlin, M. (2023). *Yes, African midwives successfully performed C-sections before it was common in Europe.* Verifythis.com. https://www.verifythis.com/article/news/verify/health-verify/african-healers-midwives-performed-cesarean-c-section-birth-in-uganda-robert-felkin/536-7f7e5d0d-4dd2-4d24-821f-935858174e15

Judaism. (2018, January 5). History.com. A&E Television Networks. https://www.history.com/topics/religion/judaism

Kadari, T. (1999a, December 31). *Deborah 2: Midrash and Aggadah.* Jewish Women's Archive. https://jwa.org/encyclopedia/article/deborah-2-midrash-and-aggadah

Kadari, T. (1999b, December 31). *Sarah: Midrash and Aggadah.* Jewish Women's Archive. https://jwa.org/encyclopedia/article/sarah-midrash-and-aggadah#:~:text=Sarah%2C%20the%20first%20of%20the

Kiesling, S. (2020, September 25). *The Human Potential Movement, up close and personal. Spirituality & Health.* https://www.spiritualityhealth.com/articles/2020/09/25/the-human-potential-movement

Kohn, S. C. (n.d.). *A short history of Buddhism*. Tricycle: The Buddhist Review. https://tricycle.org/magazine/a-short-history-of-buddhism/

Labde, A. (2021, April 21). *Women's participation In Buddhism*. Feminism in India. https://feminisminindia.com/2021/04/22/women-participation-in-buddhism/#:~:text=The%20Buddha%20emphasises%20the%20fruitful

Lakshmi. (n.d.). New World Encyclopedia. https://www.newworldencyclopedia.org/entry/lakshmi

Mani, V. (2019, January 28). *Story of Udayana*. The Wisdom Library. https://www.wisdomlib.org/hinduism/compilation/puranic-encyclopaedia/d/doc242020.html

Mark, J. (2020, June 8). *Hinduism*. World History Encyclopedia. https://www.worldhistory.org/hinduism/

Meier, K. S. (n.d.). *The beliefs of the Apache Native Americans*. Classroom.synonym.com. https://classroom.synonym.com/beliefs-apache-native-americans-6291.html

Melton, J. G. (2013). *Spiritualism religion*. In Encyclopædia Britannica. https://www.britannica.com/topic/spiritualism-religion

Melton, J. G. (2018). *Wicca - History & beliefs*. In Encyclopædia Britannica. https://www.britannica.com/topic/Wicca

Melton, J. G. (2019). *New Age movement - Religious movement*. In Encyclopædia Britannica. https://www.britannica.com/topic/New-Age-movement

Melton, J. G. (2020). *Theosophy - Definition, beliefs, history, & facts*. In Encyclopædia Britannica. https://www.britannica.com/topic/theosophy

Metzger, R. (2015, July 25). *Have you ever wondered how many Scientologists there REALLY are?* DangerousMinds. https://dangerousminds.net/comments/have_you_ever_wond ered_how_many_scientologists_there_really_are1

Nelson, T. (2020). NKJV *Abide Bible Red Letter Edition* [Stone]. Thomas Nelson.

New Thought religious movement. (n.d.). Encyclopedia Britannica. https://www.britannica.com/event/New-Thought

NÍ G, M. (n.d.). *Taoist sexuality and the feminine.* HerStory. https://www.herstory.ie/photo-essays-2/2021/9/26/taoist-sexuality-and-the-feminine

Ojukutu-Macauley, L. (2021, March 8). *Women's International Day – West African earth goddess.* Imọlẹ Candles. https://imolecandles.co.uk/blogs/news-1/women-s-international-day-west-african-earth-goddess#:~:text=Who%20is%20Ala%3F

Okunade, A. O. (2022). The role of women in African traditional religion. *The Palgrave Handbook of African Traditional Religion*, 219–229. https://doi.org/10.1007/978-3-030-89500-6_17

Olupona, J. (2014, October). 15 *facts on African religions.* OUPblog. https://blog.oup.com/2014/05/15-facts-on-african-religions/

Parvati. (2022, November 18). New World Encyclopedia. https://www.newworldencyclopedia.org/entry/Parvati#Attrib utes_and_Symbolism

Paudel, A., & Dong, Q. (2017). The Discrimination of Women in Buddhism: An Ethical Analysis. *OALib*, 04(04), 1–18. https://doi.org/10.4236/oalib.1103578

Rahman, S. (2023, January 30). *What do Buddhist nuns wear?* Budding Buddhist. https://buddingbuddhist.com/what-do-buddhist-nuns-wear/

Razwy, S. A. A. (2013, November 10). *A list of "firsts" in Islam.* Al Islam. https://www.al-islam.org/restatement-history-islam-and-muslims-sayyid-ali-asghar-razwy/list-firsts-islam

Religions - Judaism: Jewish beliefs. (2009, September 14). BBC. https://www.bbc.co.uk/religion/religions/judaism/beliefs/beliefs_1.shtml

Reninger, E. (2019, June 25). *The role of women in Taoism.* Learn Religions. https://www.learnreligions.com/gender-and-the-tao-3183069#:~:text=The%20Role%20of%20Women%20in

Rich, T. R. (n.d.). *The role of women - Judaism 101.* Judaism 101. https://www.jewfaq.org/role_of_women

Rinpoche, A. T. (2018, August 23). *The past and the future of women in Buddhism.* Buddhistdoor Global. https://www.buddhistdoor.net/features/the-past-and-the-future-of-women-in-buddhism/

Rosenlee, L.-H. (2023). *Gender in confucian philosophy.* (E. N. Zalta & U. Nodelman, Eds.). Stanford Encyclopedia of Philosophy; Metaphysics Research Lab, Stanford University. https://plato.stanford.edu/entries/confucian-gender/

Roten, J. (n.d.). *Women role models.* University of Dayton, Ohio. https://udayton.edu/imri/mary/w/women-role-models.php

Rust, B. (2022, October 22). *Is the Bible against women leading in church?* Crosswalk. https://www.crosswalk.com/church/pastors-or-leadership/is-the-bible-against-women-leading-in-church.html

Shuler, E. (2012). *A Balancing Act: A Discussion of Gender Roles Within Wiccan Ritual Ritual.* In Digital Commons. Utah State

University.
/https://digitalcommons.usu.edu/cgi/viewcontent.cgi?article=
1020&context=imwjournal

Singley, R. L. (2020, March 30). *A brief history of Islam*. Medium.
https://richardsingley.medium.com/a-brief-history-of-islam-
4dc460e0afe3

Stefon, M. (2019). *Christianity - The history of Christianity*. In
Encyclopædia   Britannica.
https://www.britannica.com/topic/Christianity/The-history-
of-Christianity

Sulomm, D. E. (2006). *The contemporary Torah : a gender-sensitive adaption of
the JPS translation*. Jewish Publ. Society.

Taoism. (2023, January 31). National Geographic Society.
https://education.nationalgeographic.org/resource/taoism/

Taoism and Confucianism - Ancient philosophies. (n.d.). US Histories.
https://www.ushistory.org/civ/9e.asp#:~:text=Confucianism
%20deals%20with%20social%20matters

Thompson, K. (2018, October 23). *Why are there more women in the New
Age Movement than men?* ReviseSociology.
https://revisesociology.com/2018/10/23/why-are-there-more-
women-in-the-new-age-movement-than-men/

Trible, P. (1999, December 31). *Miriam: Bible*. Jewish Women's Archive.
https://jwa.org/encyclopedia/article/miriam-
bible#:~:text=Miriam%20is%20best%20known%20for

Tse, L. (2007). *Tao Te Ching*. Bnpublishing.com.

Watson, B. (2007). *The Analects of Confucius*. In Columbia University
Press.   Columbia   University   Press.
http://cup.columbia.edu/book/the-analects-of-

confucius/9780231141642#:~:text=Compiled%20by%20disci
ples%20of%20Confucius

Watts, J. (1987). *Women in Buddhism.* University of Idaho.
https://www.webpages.uidaho.edu/ngier/307/women307.htm

What is the Scientology position regarding women ministers? (1 C.E., January 1).
Official Church of Scientology: What Is Scientology?
https://www.scientology.org/faq/scientology-
ministers/scientology-position-on-women-ministers.html

Why do Buddhist monks shave their heads? (n.d.). HeadBlade.
https://headblade.com/blogs/general/why-do-buddhist-
monks-shave-their-
heads#:~:text=Ridding%20of%20your%20hair%20serves

Wicca. (2019, November 6). *Defense Culture.*
https://www.defenseculture.mil/Portals/90/Documents/Tool
kit/ReligiousAwareness/FACTS-REL-Wicca-
20191106.pdf?ver=2020-01-31-142221-557

Wicca beliefs and practices. (n.d.). In University of Missouri - St Louis -
Pagan Society.
https://www.umsl.edu/~naumannj/Geography%20PowerPoi
nt%20Slides/major%20religions/other%20religions/Wicca%2
0Beliefs%20and%20Practices.pdf

Wigington, P. (2019). *Yoruba religion: History and beliefs.* Learn Religions.
https://www.learnreligions.com/yoruba-religion-4777660

Wilson, T. A. (2010). *Cult of Confucius.* Hamilton.edu.
https://academics.hamilton.edu/asian_studies/home/culttemp
/sitepages/fiveclassics.html

Women in Islam. (n.d.). The Pluralism Project - Harvard University.
https://pluralism.org/women-in-islam

Women in Tibetan Buddhism. (2021, November 8). Norbulingka Institute of Tibetan Culture. https://norbulingka.org/blogs/news-from-dharamsala/women-in-tibetan-buddhism

Women's rights and inclusion - Practices in Hinduism. (n.d.). BBC Bitesize. https://www.bbc.co.uk/bitesize/guides/zvrsv9q/revision/10#:~:text=The%20Vedas%20hold%20women%20in

Women's issues. (n.d.). NCAI. https://www.ncai.org/policy-issues/education-health-human-services/women-s-issues#:~:text=One%20cannot%20truly%20understand%20Native

Woods, K. (2019, May 18). *What does the Bible say about women?* Bible Study Tools; Salem Web Network. https://www.biblestudytools.com/bible-study/topical-studies/what-does-the-bible-say-about-women.html

Xuan Yun, Z. (n.d.). *Daoist nun – Sun Buer.* Daoist Gate. Retrieved April 28, 2023, from https://daoistgate.com/dao-sisters-sun-buer/

Zimoň, H. (2006). The Role of Women in African Traditional Religions. *Acta Ethnographica Hungarica,* 51(1-2), 43–60. https://doi.org/10.1556/aethn.51.2006.1-2.3

Image References

121821281. (2020, September 2). Zen. [Image]. Pixabay. https://pixabay.com/photos/zen-yin-yang-spirituality-harmony-5533487/

Amanda Green. (2016, July 21). Bat Mitzvah. [Image]. Pixabay. https://pixabay.com/photos/mitzvah-bar-mitzvah-sw-jewish-bat-1531490/

Arielmore. (2017, August 26). South Korea Confucian. [Image]. Pixabay. https://pixabay.com/photos/south-korea-confucian-2684103/

Cdd20. (2016, February 5). Buddha Statue. [Image]. Pixabay. https://pixabay.com/photos/buddha-statue-pond-sculpture-1177009/

D Mz. (2018, May 3). Temple Women. [Image]. Pixabay. https://pixabay.com/photos/temple-women-pillar-india-jaipur-3370930/

Dean Wittle. (2014, February 13). Native American Dancer. [Image]. Pixabay. https://pixabay.com/photos/native-american-dancer-costume-273011/

ErikaWittlieb. (2014, November 27). Confucius. [Image]. Pixabay. https://pixabay.com/photos/confucius-statue-chinese-sculpture-547153/

Gerd Altmann. (2018, January 7). Religion Question Mark. [Image]. Pixabay. https://pixabay.com/photos/religion-question-mark-analysis-3067050/

Hasyim Muhamzah. (2020, October 28). Girl Hijab. [Image]. Pixabay. https://pixabay.com/photos/girl-hijab-model-portrait-woman-5691576/

Hurk. (2014, September 23). Star of David. [Image]. Pixabay. https://pixabay.com/photos/star-of-david-star-symbol-458372/

Igor Ovyannykov. (2018, January 20). Yin Yang. [Image]. Pixabay. https://pixabay.com/photos/abstract-asia-asian-background-3092201/

Kalhh. (2017, August 25). Wicca Candle. [Image]. Pixabay. https://pixabay.com/photos/candles-space-wood-pagan-pentagram-2681068/

Manfred Antranias Zimmer. (2013, December 17). Lakshmi. [Image]. Pixabay. https://pixabay.com/photos/hinduism-gods-god-goddesses-234299/

Mohamed Hassan. (2018, April 21). Yoga Seascape. [Image]. Pixabay. https://pixabay.com/photos/yoga-sea-wave-meditation-zen-chan-3338691/

Pexels. (2016, September 11). Qur'an. [Image]. Pixabay. https://pixabay.com/photos/book-quran-open-pages-open-book-1283468/

Peter Pruzina. (2014, March 18). Wood Carving Woman. [Image]. Pixabay. https://pixabay.com/photos/wood-carving-man-woman-few-old-289005/

Rudy and Peter Skitterians. (2014, October 23). Church Altar. [Image]. Pixabay. https://pixabay.com/photos/church-altar-pews-498525/

Terrance Phiri. (2017, November 12). African Traditional Dance. [Image]. Pixabay. https://pixabay.com/photos/african-traditional-dance-2934852/

Use At Your Ease. (2016, October 27). Buddhist Nuns. [Image]. Pixabay. https://pixabay.com/photos/theravada-buddhism-buddhist-nuns-1769592/

WikiImages. (2016, August 14). Maria Holy. [Image]. Pixabay. https://pixabay.com/photos/maria-holy-maria-mother-of-god-1592567/

Made in the USA
Las Vegas, NV
10 November 2023

80585786R00075